The Land and People of
PAKISTAN

The Land and People of®
PAKISTAN

by Mark Weston

HarperCollins*Publishers*

To my mother, Marybeth Weston,
and to the Nasim family

Country maps by Philip Stickler/Stickler Cartography
Every effort has been made to locate the copyright holders of all
copyrighted materials and to secure from them the necessary
publication permissions. In the event that any questions
arise with regard to the use of copyrighted materials,
the publisher will be glad to make necessary
changes in future printings and editions.

The Land and People of Pakistan
Copyright © 1992 by James Mark Weston
Printed in the U.S.A. All rights reserved.
For information address HarperCollins Children's Books,
a division of HarperCollins Publishers,
10 East 53rd Street, New York, NY 10022.
1 2 3 4 5 6 7 8 9 10
First Edition

Library of Congress Cataloging-in-Publication Data
Weston, Mark.
     The land and people of Pakistan / by Mark Weston.
          p.   cm.
     Includes bibliographical references and index.
     Filmography: p.
     Discography: p.
     Summary: Introduces the history, geography,
people, culture, government, and economy of Pakistan.
     ISBN 0-06-022789-3. — ISBN 0-06-022790-7 (lib. bdg.)
     1. Pakistan—Juvenile literature. [1. Pakistan.]   I. Title.
II. Series.
DS376.9.W48   1992   91-2847
954.91—dc20   CIP
                                                                          AC

ACKNOWLEDGMENTS

Many people helped me write this book. I would especially like to thank my editor at HarperCollins, Marc Aronson, who was a constant help in the quest for clarity, and his assistant editor, Catharine Rigby, who guided this book through the steps to completion.

Syed Nasir Ali, Shaukat Hayat, and Anna Marie Kruizinga at Pakistan International Airlines, and Iqbal Walji, Abdul Hamid Aslam, and Amjad Ayub at Travel Walji's, helped arrange travel to parts of Pakistan that would have been difficult for me to see on my own.

Khwaja Ijaz Sarwar, Director General, Films and Publications, at Pakistan's Ministry of Information and Broadcasting, and S. Hasan Shakir Jafri, the immediate Officer-in-Charge there, helped me obtain many photographs of Pakistan. So did Margaret Riddle, Photo Librarian at the United Nations in New York.

I would also like to thank the Ragdale Foundation and the Hambidge Center for providing me with quiet and supportive places to work.

I am grateful to Dr. Mohammad Noorullah, Wheat Commissioner of Pakistan's Ministry of Food and Agriculture, and to Dr. Frances W. Pritchett, Associate Professor of Modern Indic Languages at Columbia University, for their time and insight; to Hafiz Ahrayn, of the Orangi Pilot Project in Karachi, for putting me on the back of his motorcycle and introducing me to dozens of people in Orangi; and to my sister, Carol Weston, who edited three of my chapters in spite of her own writing deadlines.

Finally, I would like to thank each member of the Nasim family in Lahore and Sahiwal—Nasim, Murzia, Anjum, Shanaz, Sanval, Savail, Azi, Aneela, and Neha—for taking me into their homes and introducing me to urban and rural life in Pakistan.

My deepest thanks go to my mother, Marybeth Weston, a rigorous editor and a fountain of encouragement and love.

Contents

THE WORLD

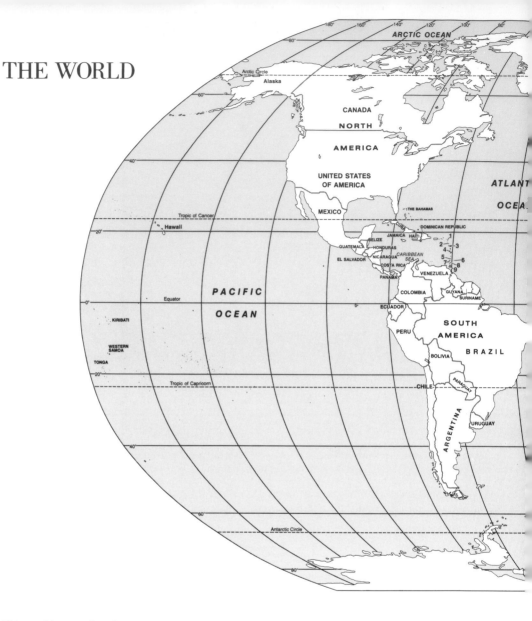

This world map is based on a projection developed by Arthur H. Robinson. The shape of each country and its size, relative to other countries, are more accurately expressed here than in previous maps. The map also gives equal importance to all of the continents, instead of placing North America at the center of the world. *Used by permission of the Foreign Policy Association.*

Legend

—— International boundaries

-------- Disputed or undefined boundaries

Projection: Robinson

0   1000   2000   3000 Miles

0   1000   2000   3000 Kilometers

Caribbean Nations

1. Anguilla
2. St. Christopher and Nevis
3. Antigua and Barbuda
4. Dominica
5. St. Lucia
6. Barbados
7. St. Vincent
8. Grenada
9. Trinidad and Tobago

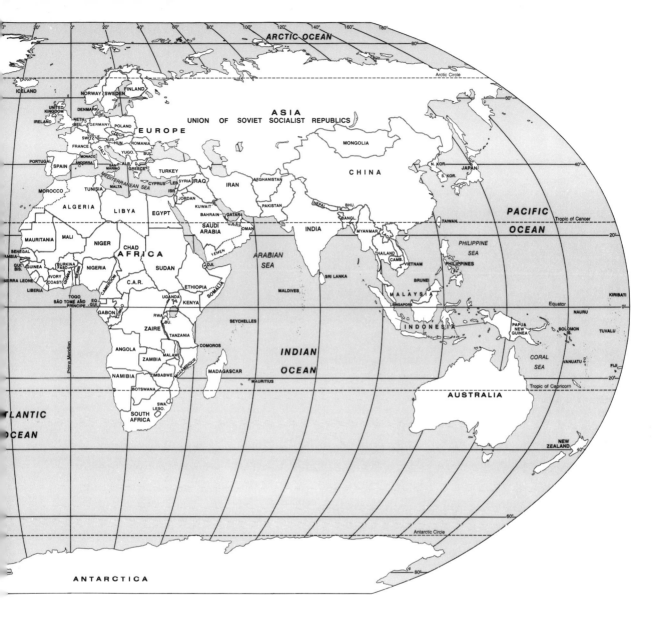

Abbreviations

ALB.	—Albania	C.A.R.	—Central African Republic	LEB.	—Lebanon	SWA.	—Swaziland
AUS.	—Austria	CZECH.	—Czechoslovakia	LESO.	—Lesotho	SWITZ.	—Switzerland
BANGL.	—Bangladesh	DJI.	—Djibouti	LIE.	—Liechtenstein	U.A.E.	—United Arab Emirates
BEL.	—Belgium	EQ. GUI.	—Equatorial Guinea	LUX.	—Luxemburg	YUGO.	—Yugoslavia
BHU.	—Bhutan	GER.	Germany	NETH.	—Netherlands		
BU.	—Burundi	GUI. BIS.	—Guinea Bissau	N. KOR.	—North Korea		
BUL.	—Bulgaria	HUN.	—Hungary	RWA.	—Rwanda		
CAMB.	—Cambodia	ISR.	—Israel	S. KOR.	—South Korea		

Mini Facts

OFFICIAL NAME: Islamic Republic of Pakistan

LOCATION: The South Asian subcontinent, also known as the Indian subcontinent. To the east of Pakistan is India, to the south the Arabian Sea, to the west Iran, to the northwest Afghanistan, and to the northeast China.

AREA: 335,356 square miles (868,591 square kilometers), about the size of Texas and Oklahoma

POPULATION: 115 million (1991 estimate), equal to about 46 percent of the population of the United States

LANGUAGES: Urdu is Pakistan's official language. It is the native language of only 8 percent of the people, but over 70 percent of Pakistanis can understand it. Over 50 percent of Pakistan's people speak Punjabi as their native language, though literate Punjabis usually read and write in Urdu rather than Punjabi.

Fourteen percent of Pakistanis speak Pashto, 12 percent Sindhi, 10 percent Saraiki, and 3 percent Baluchi. In addition, the educated elite, perhaps 3 percent of the people, are fluent in English.

RELIGION: 95 percent Muslim (75 percent Sunni, 20 percent Shia), 3 percent Christian, and 1.5 percent Hindu

CAPITAL: Islamabad, a new city built by the government in the 1960's

TYPE OF GOVERNMENT: Republic. Pakistan is currently a parliamentary democracy, but it has endured long periods of military dictatorship. Even today, no civilian government can alienate the army and stay in power for long.

HEAD OF STATE: President

HEAD OF GOVERNMENT: Prime Minister

LEGISLATURE: A National Assembly of 237 members elected every five years, or sooner if it is dissolved by the President

ADULT LITERACY: 25 percent nationwide—55 percent urban men; 35 percent urban women; 25 percent rural men; 7 percent rural women

LIFE EXPECTANCY: 52 years, male; 51 years, female (1986 estimate)

MONETARY UNIT: Rupee (March 1992: 24.7 = $1 U.S.)

AVERAGE ANNUAL PER CAPITA INCOME: Slightly over $400, less than 1/30 that of the United States

HOUSEHOLD INCOME FOR AN AVERAGE FAMILY OF SEVEN: 2,200 rupees ($90 U.S.) per month

CHIEF CROPS: Wheat, cotton, rice, sugar, millet, corn, tobacco

CHIEF INDUSTRIES: Cotton-textile manufacturing, food processing (e.g., grain milling, sugar refining, and vegetable-oil production), fertilizer production, cigarettes, carpets, steel

PAKISTAN

--- Provincial boundaries
-·-·- International boundaries
■ National capital
◘ Provincial capitals
▲ Ancient cities

| 0 | 50 | 100 | 150 | miles |
| 0 | 100 | 200 | km |

AFGHANISTAN

PAKISTAN

IRAN

CHINA

BANGLADESH

INDIA

U.S.S.R.

CHINA

NORTHERN AREAS

GILGIT AGENCY

Gilgit

BALTIT AGENCY

Swat Valley

1972 CEASEFIRE LINE

AZAD KASHMIR

Khyber Pass

WEST PROVINCE

FEDERALLY ADMINISTERED TRIBAL AREAS

NORTH-WEST FRONTIER

Peshawar

■ISLAMABAD

Rawalpindi

Sialkot

LAHORE ◘

Faisalabad

Harappa ▲

Multan

PUNJAB

Bahawalpur

Quetta ◘

Sibi

BALUCHISTAN

INDIA

Sukkur

Larkana

Mohenjodaro ▲

SIND

Gwador

Hyderabad

KARACHI ◘

Thatta

Thar Desert

ARABIAN SEA

Introduction

One out of every fifty human beings is a Pakistani. With 115 million people, Pakistan has almost half the population of the United States. It is one of the ten most populous nations on earth.

Pakistan is also one of the few nations in the world capable of making nuclear weapons. In 1986 Pakistani scientists finished building the components of several atomic bombs, making Pakistan the first Islamic nation to be a nuclear power.

Pakistan is a new nation, formed as a Muslim homeland in 1947. But people have lived within its boundaries since the Indus River civilization flourished 4,500 years ago.

Pakistan is a male-dominated nation in which millions of women are confined to the home, and only 15 percent of adult women can read and write. But Pakistan also has many female doctors, lawyers, and teachers, and from 1988 to 1990 its prime minister was a woman.

Compared to the United States, Pakistan is a poor nation. The typical villager is a farmer who lives in a mud-walled house and laboriously plows land with an ox. But even the poor in Pakistan have enough to eat, and when they cook a special meal, they enjoy one of the most delicious and sophisticated cuisines on the planet.

The terrain of Pakistan includes five of the world's seventeen highest mountains, a vast desert, the largest irrigation network in the world, and hundreds of miles of almost uninhabited beaches.

The cities of Pakistan appear to host several centuries simulta-

Tens of thousands of Pakistanis pray during the holiday of Eid al-Fitr *at the Badshahi mosque in Lahore, the second-largest mosque in the world.* Pakistan Directorate of Films and Publications

Motorcycles roar past a movie theater on a busy street in Karachi. Mark Weston

neously. In crowded bazaars, bells jingle as horses pull veiled women in carts past spice merchants wearing turbans and street vendors cooking shish kebabs. But in the skies, the jets of Pakistan International Airlines fly over many blocks of new office buildings and apartment houses.

Few countries are as representative of the developing world as Pakistan, and this makes it particularly rewarding to study. Although Pakistan is one of the poorest nations outside of Africa, it is wealthier than China, India, and Bangladesh. Personal income in Pakistan is very close to the world median.

Pakistan is also representative of a large portion of the developing

A Note on Pronunciation

In Urdu, the national language of Pakistan, Pakistan means "the land of the pure." It is properly pronounced pahk-ih-STAHN. Only in America, where an "ah" usually sounds affected, is the country's name pronounced PACK-ih-stan.

world because it is a hybrid of two great civilizations, that of India and that of Islam. Through the centuries Pakistan has belonged to empires stretching east across India as far as Bangladesh, and west across Arabia as far as Morocco. Anyone who reads about Pakistan also learns about this vast area that contains more than a quarter of the world's people.

The story of Pakistan is the story of the Muslims in India—how they arrived as conquerors, gradually spoke new languages, built fabulous mosques and palaces, and converted millions of Hindus to Islam. It is also the story of how Muslims lived with Hindus yet remained distinct from, and were finally fearful of, the Hindus. Before the British left India in 1947, the Muslims demanded a nation of their own.

Three hundred million Muslims live on the South Asian subcontinent today, more than all the people in the Middle East and North Africa combined. Over a third of these Muslims live in Pakistan, the only modern nation besides Israel intentionally formed as a religious homeland.

The Land

Pakistan is where the mountains and deserts of Central Asia descend to meet the fertile lowlands of India. It is today, as it has been for centuries, a crossroads where the herdsmen of the mountains trade goods and swap stories with the farmers and townspeople of the plains.

The boundary between the dry mountains of the west and the fertile farmland of the east is the Indus River. Beginning in a lake in Tibet, the Indus River runs 1,800 miles (2,900 kilometers) through the length of Pakistan, south to the Arabian Sea. Many tributaries along the way add their waters to the Indus, and together they form a river system that provides water to two thirds of Pakistan.

If it were not for the Indus and its tributaries, Pakistan's scorching subtropical sun would long ago have turned the whole nation into a desert. The monsoon, a series of storms, moves from the Bay of Bengal northwest across India every summer, but it peters out by the time it gets to Pakistan, and there is little rain during the rest of the year.

In most of the world land is fertile because storms provide the soil with sufficient rain. In Pakistan, land is fertile primarily because people have worked hard to build and maintain over eighty-five thousand canals, irrigation ditches, and tube wells. Indeed, it is a tribute to the industry of the farmers of Pakistan that, in a nation so dry and dusty, they can feed all 115 million of their people.

Geography

Not including the autonomous area of Azad Kashmir, Pakistan covers 335,356 square miles (868,591 square kilometers). This is about the size of Texas and Oklahoma combined, or the states and provinces of the Atlantic coast from Nova Scotia to North Carolina. Pakistan lies east of Iran, north of the Arabian Sea, west of India, southwest of China, and southeast of Afghanistan.

In 1981 the Soviet Union quietly annexed Afghanistan's mountainous northeastern panhandle, known as the Wakhan Corridor, and it is unknown whether the Soviets actually left this remote but strategic region when they withdrew from the rest of Afghanistan in 1989. So today Pakistan may also have a 150-mile (240-kilometer) border with the once-Soviet republic of Tajikistan.

Five provinces make up Pakistan: the Punjab, the flat farmland where over half of Pakistan's people live; Sind, a desert, but with the fertile Indus River valley running through; the North-West Frontier Province, a land of arid peaks, narrow valleys, and a fierce, tribal people; Baluchistan, a high and vast desert with little water and few people; and the Northern Areas, land that Pakistan disputes with India, a spectacular land of glaciers, steep gorges, and some of the highest mountains in the world.

THE LAND

U.S.S.R.

IRAN

U.S.S.R

CHINA

AFGHANISTAN

Hindu Kush Mts.

Hunza Valley

Karakoram Mts.

K2

Gilgit

Himalaya Mts.

Kabul R.

Safed Koh

Islamabad

Potwar Plateau

Indus R.

Jhelum R.

Chenab R.

Beas R.

Lahore

Ravi R.

Quetta

Sulaiman Range

Sutlej R.

Baluchistan Plateau

Sui Gas Field

IRAN

Kirthar Range

Indus R.

INDIA

Makran Coast Range

Hyderabad

Thar Desert

Karachi

ARABIAN SEA

| 0 | 50 | 100 | 150 miles |
| 0 | 100 | 200 | km |

The Punjab

The heart of Pakistan is the Punjab, the grassy plain that lies primarily east of the Indus River and south of the Himalayan foothills. The Punjab was divided between India and Pakistan in 1947, but two thirds of it was awarded to Pakistan. Today, the province is home to almost 70 million Pakistanis, a majority of the nation. Four and a half million live in Lahore, Pakistan's cultural center and second largest city.

In Sanskrit, the ancient language of India, the name Punjab means "five rivers," for there are five tributaries east of the Indus River. These are the Chenab, Jhelum, Ravi, Sutlej, and Beas rivers. The re-

Children bathe and do laundry by a tube well.   United Nations/Carl Purcell

A farmer in the Punjab opens an irrigation ditch to water his wheat crop. United Nations/K. Muldoon

gional name Punjab and our English word "pentagon" both come from the same root, *pancha*, which is the Sanskrit word for "five."

The "land of five rivers" is almost as flat as a table. Follow any of the riverbanks from north to south, and the grassland slopes downward only one foot per mile (less than 20 centimeters per kilometer). Even if one crosses the center of the Punjab from east to west, no land is ever more than 40 feet (12 meters) higher than a nearby river.

Size and Population of Pakistan's Provinces

Province	Square Miles	Square Kilometers	Estimated Population	Comparable Statistics
Punjab (including Islamabad)	79,632	206,250	67 million	Size of Kansas. Rainfall of western Kansas. Population of midwest U.S.
Sind	54,407	140,914	26 million	34% size of California. Rainfall of San Diego, California. Population of California.
Baluchistan	134,050	347,190	5.5 million	20% bigger than Nevada. Rainfall of Nevada. Population of Arizona and Nevada.

The flatness of the Punjab has allowed its people to transform it into the most extensively irrigated area in the world. Over 80 percent of the farmland in the Punjab is irrigated. Water reaches crops not only through canals and ditches, but also through tube wells. In a tube well, an electric motor pumps water up through a pipe and then out into nar-

North-West Frontier Province	39,282	101,741	16 million	Half the size of Wyoming. Rainfall of Wyoming. Population of U.S. Rocky Mountain states.
(Tribal Areas)	*10,509*	*27,220*	*3 million*	*30% bigger than Wales. Population of Wales.*
Northern Areas	27,985	72,496	600,000	Size of New Brunswick, Canada. Rainfall of New Mexico. Population of New Brunswick, Canada.
Total Pakistan	335,356	868,591	115 million	Size of Texas and Oklahoma. 46% population of U.S.

row, brick-lined channels that run between fields.

Irrigation is crucial because rainfall in most of the Punjab is less than 20 inches (50 centimeters) per year, about that of western Kansas or the driest parts of Spain. In the southern third of the Punjab, it rains only 7 inches (18 centimeters) a year, about the average rainfall of Arizona.

Most of this rain comes only during the summer monsoon. During the rest of the year, a farmer's only reliable source of water is a tube well or an irrigation ditch.

Some farms in the Punjab are quite large, but most are small, averaging just 13 acres (5.25 hectares). A typical farmer and his family plant wheat in October or November and water it regularly during the mild but dry winter. In late April, men and women work well into the evening to harvest the wheat, for by early May, temperatures sometimes rise as high as 110°F (43°C). Wheat is Pakistan's main crop, and three fourths of it is grown in the Punjab.

During the arid months of May and June, grass turns brown, acacia trees grow heavy with dust, water buffaloes become sluggish, and irrigation ditches run low. At last, around the first of July, the black clouds of the monsoon roll in from the Indian Ocean amid thunder and lightning. For two months, while farmers grow a second crop, usually cotton or rice, dozens of torrential downpours fill up rivers, canals, and ditches, and sometimes cause floods. The rains ensure that next year there will once again be enough water to grow wheat during the dry winter.

In the northern Punjab, west of the Jhelum River, is the Potwar Plateau, a low-lying area of dry hills and small canyons much like the badlands of South Dakota. It extends west to the Indus River and north to the pine-covered foothills of the Himalayas. The region includes Islamabad, the newly built capital of Pakistan, and its older and larger twin city, Rawalpindi. The Potwar Plateau is not as fertile as the rest of the Punjab, so many villagers there engage in sheepherding, or leave the land altogether to join the army.

Because the Punjab is so very flat, and because it is not far from the Khyber Pass on Afghanistan's border, Muslim armies from Afghanistan found the Punjab to be an easy region to conquer. Their many invasions over the centuries led more people to convert to Islam in the Punjab than in other regions of the South Asian subcontinent. This high proportion of Muslims in the Punjab became one of the major reasons for the partition of India and the creation of Pakistan in 1947.

In the southern Punjab, the "five rivers" merge together and then, a few miles later, join the Indus. Seventy-five miles (120 kilometers) south of this junction, the Indus River, now over a mile wide, quietly leaves the Punjab and flows into Sind.

Sind

Almost one quarter of Pakistan's people live in Sind, the nation's southeastern province. The 26 million people of Sind are as dependent upon the Indus River as the people of Egypt are upon the Nile. Near the Indus there are lush fields of wheat, cotton, and rice, luxuriant groves of date palms, and orchards so heavy with fruit that farmers must prop the branches up with wooden beams.

But move away from the Indus and the land is dry, dusty, and covered only with scrub. Less than 75 miles (120 kilometers) west of the Indus is the bone-dry plateau of Baluchistan. The same distance east of the Indus are the towering sand dunes of the vast Thar Desert, most of which lies across the border in India.

The name Sind comes from "Sindhu," the Sanskrit word for the Indus River. Persian conquerors in the sixth century B.C. had difficulty aspirating the "s" and sometimes dropped it, and from this new pronunciation came the words "Hindu," "India," "Indus," and, in America many centuries later, "Indian" and "Indiana."

Winters in Sind are pleasant and warm, but in the summer the average temperature is a blistering 90°F (32°C). Many homeowners in Sind put wind chutes on their roofs, so that if there is even a slight breeze it will funnel down inside the home.

Rainfall in Sind is even less than in the Punjab, averaging under 10 inches (25 centimeters) a year, an amount about equal to that of New Mexico. In the summer, the monsoon barely touches the northern half of Sind, which receives less than 5 inches (13 centimeters) of rain a year. In Sind, water comes from the Indus, not from the sky.

Men and women have farmed along the Indus for over 4,500 years, and during all that time the slow-moving river has been carrying and then depositing dirt and clay and sand. The riverbed of the lower Indus is now higher than the nearby fields, so farmers have built and maintained levees that go on for long distances.

The people of Sind have also constructed irrigation networks throughout the province nearly as extensive as those in the Punjab. These waterways allow farmers to grow crops many miles from the Indus. Some farmers in eastern Sind even plant fields in the Thar Desert.

Unfortunately, in recent years water has seeped through the soil of many irrigation canals in Sind and raised the water table—the level of underground water—making some soil so waterlogged that it is useless for farming. Worse, when the waterlogged soil dries out, there are deposits of salts that make it impossible for plants to grow.

Waterlogging and salinity occur in the Punjab too, but it is worse in Sind, where thousands of acres of land are being ruined monthly. Pumping water up from tube wells lowers the water table and washes salts away, but the construction of enough tube wells to relieve this problem will take a long time and a lot of money.

As the Indus River approaches the Arabian Sea, it fans out to form a delta. The water in the delta is brown with silt, and much of the swampy land is underwater during high tide. To the west of the Indus Delta is Karachi, Pakistan's largest city. Karachi is the seaport and commercial center of Pakistan, and it is home to over nine million people. It is also less than 20 miles (32 kilometers) from the border of Baluchistan.

Baluchistan

Baluchistan is the largest, driest, poorest, and most sparsely populated province in Pakistan. Its five and a half million people are spread across 44 percent of Pakistan's land area, but they comprise only 5 percent of the nation's people. Most of Baluchistan is a vast plateau, stretching from the mountains of Afghanistan in the north to the Arabian Sea in the south, and from the border of Iran in the west to the Kirthar mountain range in the east. The Kirthar mountains, west of the Indus River, form Baluchistan's boundary with Sind province. They are only about 6,000 feet (1,800 meters) high.

The Baluchistan Plateau is an inhospitable land of dry lakes and riverbeds interspersed with steep hills and barren mountains. It is 2,000 to 3,000 feet (600 to 900 meters) high, high enough so that in winter the nighttime temperature is well below freezing. Summers on the plateau are very hot. Dust storms are common, and sometimes there is a scorching summer wind known as the *juloh* ("flame"), which can kill even hardy desert plants that lie in its path.

The colors of Baluchistan are shades of brown: parched earth, barren mountains, mud-walled villages, and dust filling the skies and settling on the faces and clothes of the people.

In the west, neighboring Iran has its own province named Baluchistan. In both the Persian and the Baluchi languages, Baluchistan means "Land of the Baluch," after the nomadic people who inhabit this region.

To the east, Baluchistan's border is roughly 60 miles (100 kilometers) west of the Indus River, far enough so only a few canals in Baluchistan draw water from the river's irrigation system. Unfortunately, Baluchistan is also completely outside the path of the summer monsoon, so the province receives almost no water at all.

A camel helps a farmer plow the parched soil of Baluchistan. United Nations

Without water, there is little agriculture in Baluchistan. A few lakes and oases support some wheat fields, almond groves, and apricot orchards, especially in the valley around Quetta, Baluchistan's capital city. But in most of Baluchistan, the only way to make a living from the harsh land is to herd sheep and goats.

Baluchistan has virtually no industry, except for some mines near the Afghan border (mostly coal, chromite, marble, and onyx) and some woolen mills and hide tanneries. Having so few farms and factories, Baluchistan also has very few towns and, except for Quetta, no cities.

To the northeast, Baluchistan's border with the Punjab is formed by the Sulaiman mountains. They are relatively low mountains, rarely rising over 6,000 feet (1,800 meters) high. But at the south of the Sulaiman range, at the foot of the Bugti hills, is Pakistan's most important source of fuel, the Sui gas fields.

Sui is just across the border from the Punjab. Farther west, the mineral potential of most of Baluchistan remains unexplored. Baluchistan is so big that it is almost certain that somewhere in the province an adventurous geologist will discover more gas fields, or perhaps some valuable mineral deposits.

South of the Baluchistan Plateau, just inland from the Arabian Sea, is the Makran Coast range. These mountains are not high, but they are so steep that they have isolated Baluchistan's coastline from the rest of Pakistan. In this region, known as the Makran Coast, all of the rivers dry up when the rain stops. As a result, the Makran Coast has no cities, resorts, or towns of any size—only 300 miles (480 kilometers) of deserted beaches, one small port, and about a dozen fishing villages.

The North-West Frontier Province

Northeast of Baluchistan, but northwest of the rest of the South Asian subcontinent, is a province that the British created in 1901, the North-West Frontier Province. Home to over 16 million people, the Frontier begins across the Indus River from the Punjab, and gradually climbs upward through dry and craggy hills until it reaches the mountainous border of Afghanistan.

The N.W.F.P., as it is sometimes called for short, is very much a frontier, in both its geography and its spirit. In the colonial era, when Britain ruled everything from what is now Bangladesh to the Afghan border, the Province was the northwesternmost outpost of British India, the frontier of British rule along the mountains of Central Asia. Beyond the North-West Frontier Province lay Afghanistan, which was then, as it is today, a buffer state between Russia and the subcontinent.

The North-West Frontier Province is the home of the well-armed and fiercely independent Pakhtun people. The mountainous terrain of their homeland makes it impossible for any nation to fully conquer them. If an army invades a valley, the Pakhtuns can flee to the hills. If the army marches up the hills in pursuit, the Pakhtuns can ambush them.

As a result, the government of Pakistan limits its authority in the Frontier to the cities, valleys, and major passes, and lets the Pakhtuns in the mountains run their own affairs. The government designates more than one fourth of the land inside the North-West Frontier Province as Tribal Areas. Here the government collects no taxes, and its laws have no force. Even if a Pakhtun decides to grow poppies and manufacture opium and heroin—and many do—the Pakistani police will not interfere. The only authority in a tribal area is the local council, or *jirga*.

The best known of the tribal areas is the Khyber Agency, home of the Khyber Pass, the most famous mountain pass in the world. Since the time of Alexander the Great, armies have used this pass because it is the widest and lowest of the mountain routes from Afghanistan into India. The winding road is never more than 3,500 feet (1,100 meters) high, and its eastern end is only 25 miles (40 kilometers) from Peshawar, the Frontier's largest city.

Both the Khyber Pass and the city of Peshawar are not far from the Kabul River. This river flows east from Kabul, the capital of Afghanistan, and north of the Safed Koh mountains, which are 12,000 to 16,000 feet high (3,700 to 4,900 meters) and form the border between Afghanistan and the southern half of the N.W.F.P. The Kabul River then flows east into Pakistan and across the Frontier until it joins the Indus.

The area surrounding the Kabul River is known as the Peshawar Valley, and it is the most fertile and populous part of the North-West Frontier. Over a million refugees from the war in Afghanistan have settled here. Farmers in the Peshawar Valley grow a variety of crops, including wheat, corn, apples, sugarcane, and oilseeds. Carpenters cut timber brought down from the mountains, and shopkeepers take tobacco grown in nearby fields and pound it until it is ready for sale.

South of Peshawar, and south of the high peaks of the Safed Koh, are the smaller, sun-baked mountains of Waziristan, home of the Wazirs,

Pakistani soldiers guard the Khyber Pass.   UN Photo #156462/J. Isaac

who have the reputation of being the most violent of all the Pakhtuns. These mountains are generally 5,000 to 7,000 feet (1,500 to 2,100 meters) high, although some peaks are higher.

Hot summers ensure that the dry mountains of Waziristan are brown and barren, but winters in these mountains are cold, as are nights and mornings early in the spring and late in the fall. The Wazirs, who herd large flocks of sheep and goats, have no trouble keeping warm. Like most people on the Frontier in winter, they wear a variety of wool coats, sweaters, and caps.

North of Peshawar are the cool, fertile valleys of Swat, Dir, and Chitral. Farmers here grow wheat, rice, and corn in small plots terraced against steep, pine-topped hillsides. In the spring, apple orchards and fields of mustard burst into color. These valleys are especially beautiful because they are in the foothills of the snow-capped Hindu Kush. ("Kush" is a corruption of the Persian word for "mountains.") Some of these lofty mountains are over 20,000 feet (6,000 meters) high, and they form the boundary that separates the North-West Frontier Province from Afghanistan and the remote Wakhan Corridor. But as awesome as the Hindu Kush are, they are overshadowed by the adjacent mountains of the Northern Areas.

The Northern Areas

The Northern Areas are the most visually stunning part of Pakistan. They have five of the world's seventeen highest mountains, and such extensive glaciers that the region is sometimes called "the third pole."

Most of the Northern Areas are a part of Kashmir, the province that Pakistan disputes with India. It is a spectacular land of icy peaks, high waterfalls, steep gorges, narrow valleys, and sheep famous for their fine cashmere wool. Pakistan and India both claim all of Kashmir, and fought wars over the province in 1948 and 1965. Today India holds two thirds of Kashmir, including its most beautiful lakes.

The government of Pakistan administers most of its third of Kashmir directly, having set up two territories known as the Gilgit Agency and the Baltit Agency. Together, these two agencies are known as the Northern Areas, and they are home to 600,000 people.

The remainder of Pakistani Kashmir is known as Azad Kashmir, which in the Kashmiri language means "Free Kashmir." Azad Kashmir was formed in 1948 by Muslims who opposed Indian rule in Kashmir. More than forty years later, they still work for the day when Kashmir will be united and governed by its Muslim majority. Today, Azad Kashmir is a self-governing territory, somewhat independent, but under the military protection and political influence of Pakistan.

The dominant geographical feature of the Northern Areas is the Karakoram mountain range, which spreads across most of the region. Of the world's fourteen mountains over 26,246 feet (8,000 meters) high, three are in the Karakoram range. The highest of these, called simply "K-2," sits on the border of Pakistan and China. K-2 is the second highest mountain in the world, 28,250 feet (8,611 meters) high. This is almost twice as high as Mount Whitney, the highest mountain in the contiguous United States. Even an average peak in the Karakorams is over 19,000 feet (5,800 meters) high.

A fourth high Pakistani mountain, Nanga Parbat, 26,660 feet (8,126 meters) high, is part of the Himalayan mountain range, which extends from India through Azad Kashmir, and up to the Indus River. The Himalayan mountains block the summer monsoon from reaching the Northern Areas, so the region is as dry as New Mexico or Morocco, getting only about 6 to 12 inches (15 to 30 centimeters) of rain per year.

The mountains of the Northern Areas are barren of plant life, but they are covered with glaciers. In the spring and summer, the partial

A shepherd tends his flock in the Himalayan mountains in the Northern Areas.
Mark Weston

melting of these glaciers gives rise to high waterfalls and rushing rapids. These rapids swiftly tumble down into the Indus and Jhelum rivers, and the mountain waters eventually irrigate the wheat fields of the Punjab.

The Indus River cuts a steep gorge through the center of the Northern Areas, and in many regions the only way to cross the river is by a swinging footbridge. North of the Indus, two tributaries wind through fertile valleys, and one of them, the Hunza Valley, is world famous for its beauty. Beneath spectacular snow-capped mountains, the farmers of Hunza carefully terrace steep hillsides, planting wheat fields and apricot orchards and irrigating them with glacier water. One of the most beautiful places in Pakistan, the Hunza Valley was the model for the mythical kingdom of Shangri-La in James Hilton's novel *Lost Horizon*.

Until the 1970's, the only way to reach Hunza on the ground was by mule train, or in a jeep with many spare tires and parts. But Hunza's isolation ended in 1978, when the Chinese and Pakistani armies completed the Karakoram highway. This new road has brought to Hunza and other valleys some facets of modern life, such as refrigerators, health clinics, and better schools.

The Karakoram highway stretches from Islamabad, in the Punjab, to Kashgar, in Sinkiang, China. The highway is just an undivided two-lane road, but it is a wonder that it was built at all. American engineering firms said it couldn't be done. Yet for 800 miles (1,300 kilometers) the highway twists and turns through high river gorges, hugging the edge of one almost-vertical mountainside after another.

Avalanches and falling boulders killed more than four hundred workers during the construction of the highway, and landslides continue to block traffic daily. To keep the highway open, the government of Pakistan stations bulldozers every twenty miles, just to clear the debris.

The Karakoram highway is vital to the military security of Pakistan. If war breaks out in Kashmir again, China can send Pakistan tanks, artillery, and trucks full of weapons to use against their common enemy, India.

CHAPTER III

The People and Their Languages

A Pakistani in a foreign country may say, "I am a Muslim and a Pakistani." But inside Pakistan, where 95 percent of the people are Muslims, most Pakistanis are more likely to think of themselves as belonging to a region—especially since each major region in Pakistan has its own language. The 115 million people of Pakistan can be divided into five major groups: Punjabis, Sindhis, Mohajirs, Pakhtuns, and Baluch.

Punjabis

Over 60 percent of Pakistan's people are Punjabis. Like many Pakistanis, the Punjabis are generally tall, with light-brown skin, dark hair, and brown eyes, although of course there are many variations from this norm. Most Punjabis are hard-working farmers, growing wheat and cotton on their own small plots of land.

Many Punjabis are soldiers; almost 80 percent of Pakistan's army is Punjabi. Because Pakistan's government since independence has often been a military dictatorship, the inhabitants of Sind and Baluchistan have often felt like colonized people, their provinces occupied by a Punjabi army. This feeling is weaker in the North-West Frontier

A Punjabi woman makes pottery at home.   Mark Weston

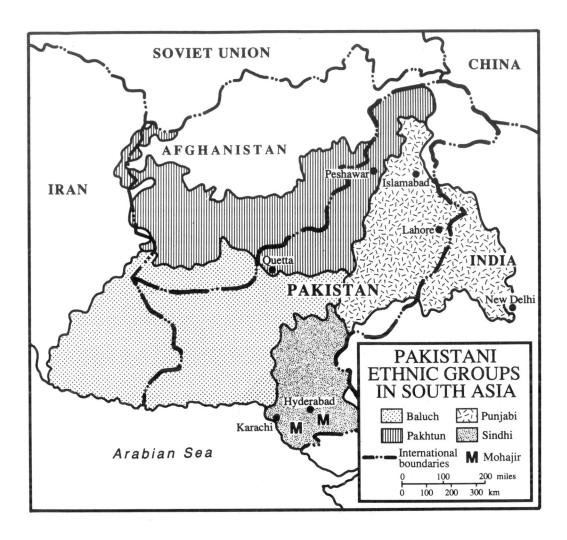

PAKISTANI ETHNIC GROUPS IN SOUTH ASIA

Baluch   Punjabi

Pakhtun   Sindhi

International boundaries   **M** Mohajir

0	100		200 miles
0	100	200	300 km

Province, however, because almost 20 percent of the army is made up of Pakhtuns from this region.

In Lahore, there is a highly educated Punjabi aristocracy and upper middle class. Lahore was briefly a center of the Mughal empire, and today it is the intellectual and cultural center of Pakistan.

Punjabis are also known for being practical and energetic businessmen, and for being frank almost to the point of rudeness. Punjabi is an earthy, informal language, rich in the idiom of rural life and full of imaginative curses. Many Punjabis, like many New Yorkers, often enjoy the use of strong language for its own sake.

Three fifths of Pakistan's people speak Punjabi, a language related to Sanskrit. Punjabi has a rich oral tradition of poems and folk songs, and many of these stories are about ill-fated young lovers—Asian counterparts to Romeo and Juliet.

Although many songs and poems are still written in Punjabi, there are very few Punjabi books, magazines, or newspapers. (In India, followers of the Sikh religion read and write Punjabi in a script called Gurmukhi, but it is a script few Muslims learn.) When Muslim Punjabis read and write, they usually do so in Urdu, the national language of Pakistan, a language closely related to Punjabi.

Sindhis

Sindhis make up 12 percent of Pakistan's population, and half of the population of Sind province. Physically, Sindhis are similar to Punjabis, although on average they may be slightly darker in complexion. Most Sindhis live in rural areas, and about half of the villagers in Sind are tenant farmers. They work in scorching heat to grow wheat, cotton, and rice on irrigated land that they do not own.

Many Sindhis are easygoing and soft-spoken, but these charming qualities developed under adversity, as a way to cope with poverty and oppression. Isolated from the rest of the subcontinent by the Thar Desert, the landlords of Sind were for centuries among the harshest in the region. Until very recently they commanded absolute obedience from their tenants, and even today their local authority is rarely questioned. Their estates are larger, the terms they give their tenant farmers are less generous, and the punishments they administer are more severe than those of landlords in other provinces.

Ordinary Sindhis therefore have had less reason to work hard and more reason to be tactful and outwardly deferential than people in other parts of Pakistan. But many of the qualities that make Sindhis pleasant to be with have hurt them economically. Sindhis today are poorer than the generally more dynamic and better-educated people who have recently come to Sind, the Mohajirs. These differences have led to violent clashes between the two groups.

Sometimes Sindhis and Mohajirs have shot each other in the streets of Karachi and Hyderabad, killing dozens at a time. And in the countryside, several thousand Sindhis have become bandits who rob and kidnap people at night. Ironically, while Sindhis have gentle manners, Sind is by far Pakistan's most violent province.

Sindhis at the tomb of Shah Abdul Latif, generally considered the greatest poet of the Sindhi language. Pakistan Directorate of Films and Publications

Unlike Punjabis, who read and write Urdu, Sindhis more often read and write their own language, Sindhi. The Arabs ruled Sind in the eighth, ninth, and tenth centuries, so the Sindhi language, which like Punjabi and Urdu is related to Sanskrit, contains many Arabic words and uses an Arabic script.

Sindhi is close enough to Urdu for most Sindhis to understand Urdu, but they prefer to use their own soft and lyrical language. Indeed, Sindhis require that their language be taught in all the public schools in Sind, including those in Karachi, where few Sindhis live. The Mohajirs, who are in the majority in Karachi, would rather spend their extra time learning English, not Sindhi.

Mohajirs

Unlike other ethnic groups in Pakistan, the Mohajirs (which in both Urdu and Arabic means "refugees") have no common racial features or character traits. The parents and grandparents of today's Mohajirs came to Pakistan in the late 1940's from cities all over India, and the only thing they had in common was a desire to live in the new Muslim nation. Only 8 percent of Pakistan's people are Mohajirs, but they include just over 50 percent of the people in Karachi and Hyderabad, Pakistan's largest and fifth-largest cities, respectively.

The Mohajirs are the only people in Pakistan who speak Urdu as a native language. Because they have lived in cities for several generations, they are also better educated and often more sophisticated than most Pakistanis. Mohajirs therefore hold a disproportionate share of jobs in business, finance, and government, much to the anger of the Sindhis, who resent their success.

In the 1970's, the Sindhis succeeded in getting the federal government to reduce the Mohajirs' share of new jobs in the civil service. To

The Major Peoples of Pakistan

Ethnic Group	Approx. Population	Approx. % of Nation	Languages
Punjabis	70 million	61%	Punjabi, Saraiki
Pakhtuns	16 million	14%	Pashto
Sindhis	14 million	12%	Sindhi
Mohajirs	9 million	8%	Urdu
Baluch	4 million	3.5%	Baluchi, Brahui

the Sindhis this was an attempt to reclaim control over their own province, but to poor and lower-middle-class Mohajirs it was an unfair quota.

In protest, the Mohajirs formed their own political party in 1985, the "Mohajir Qaumi (National) Movement." Today the MQM controls the city governments of Karachi and Hyderabad, about a dozen seats in the National Assembly, and ominously, a private army of 12,000 young men. The flag of the MQM flies on rooftops all over Karachi, marking out turf in a manner reminiscent of gangs in some American cities. One of the slogans of the MQM is "Sell your TV and buy a gun!"

The Mohajirs want Karachi to secede from Sind and become a separate province, but this is unlikely to happen. The docks and factories of Karachi are too great a source of tax revenue for the rest of the nation to entrust them to the MQM.

Karachi is the melting pot of the entire nation. The Mohajirs make up half of the city, but the remaining half of Karachi's population is divided fairly evenly among all of Pakistan's other ethnic groups. For example, one seventh of the people of Karachi, including most of the city's bus drivers and shopkeepers, are Pakhtuns, the people from the North-West Frontier Province.

Pakhtuns

If the Spartans of ancient Greece or the Klingons of *Star Trek* were to visit earth today, they might well choose to live among the Pakhtun people. Warlike, hardworking, and passionately devoted to their honor, the Pakhtuns make up 14 percent of Pakistan's population, and 45 percent of sparsely populated Afghanistan as well.

The Pakhtuns (pronounced pahk-TOONS) are also commonly known as Pathans (puh-TAHNS); this pronunciation is used by the Punjabis, the Hindus, and the British. Another version of the name is Pushtuns, a pronunciation used in much of Afghanistan and in the southern end of the North-West Frontier Province. Most of the people of the North-West Frontier, however, call themselves Pakhtuns.

The typical Pakhtun family grows wheat on its own land, and may also tend a small orchard and keep some sheep and goats. On the average, Pakhtuns are slightly lighter skinned than most Punjabis and Sindhis, although many have dark and piercing eyes. Some Pakhtuns, though, have blue eyes and even red hair. Many blue-eyed Pakhtuns claim to be descendants of the European soldiers who fought for Alexander the Great two thousand years ago.

Pakhtuns are famous throughout the subcontinent for their code of honor, the *pakhtunwali* (way of the Pakhtuns). The best-known dictate of this code is "revenge at any cost." If an enemy kills your brother, then honor demands that you kill several members of his family in return. By such escalation feuds go on for years, and the quest for revenge can pass from father to son.

Almost all Pakhtun men own rifles, and today many own machine guns too. There is a saying that a Punjabi with money buys a television set, but a Pakhtun with money buys a gun. In the Tribal Areas some Pakhtuns even own light artillery.

The wildness of the Pakhtuns has made them almost impossible to conquer. Even today, Pakistani laws and taxes do not apply in the mountainous Tribal Areas of the Frontier. The Pakhtuns there govern themselves through local tribal councils called *jirga*s. If there is a murder, or if a family feud has grown too violent, a *jirga* may mediate and make peace.

The second dictate of the code of the Pakhtuns is to provide hospitality to all strangers and guests. This obligation, which even urban Pakhtuns respect, is one of the two principal reasons why more than 3 million refugees from the war in Afghanistan during the 1980's have been able to live and work in Pakistan with so little trouble. (The other reason is the common ethnic heritage of the Pakhtuns on both sides of the Afghan–Pakistani border.)

Even the poorest Pakhtun village has a guest house so a visitor can be accommodated easily. Hosts, no matter how powerful they are, serve meals with their own hands and sit with their guests as equals.

The duty of hospitality takes precedence over the demand for revenge. If an enemy comes seeking refuge or safe passage, it must be given. It is a great humiliation, however, for a Pakhtun to ask for refuge from an enemy. (For a more detailed discussion of the Pakhtun code of honor, see *The Land and People of Afghanistan*.)

Many Pakhtuns are highly devout Muslims, praying five times a day, fasting during the month of Ramazan (or Ramadan, as the Arabs pronounce it), and giving often to the poor. Pakhtuns are also more likely than other Pakistanis to maintain the tradition of *purdah*, confining women to the home. Along a busy street in the Frontier it is common to see no women at all. When women do venture out of the house, most, though not all, wear a *burqa*, a tentlike cloth (of any color) that covers them from head to toe except for a small, net-like mesh at the center of the face. To a Westerner, a woman wearing a *burqa* looks like a Halloween ghost, but many women think the *burqa* protects their modesty from the gaze of unfamiliar men. Women wear *burqa*s throughout Pakistan, but a much higher proportion of women wear them in the North-West Frontier Province and in Baluchistan.

A Pakhtun man guards the honor of the women in his family jealously. If he suspects his wife, sister, or daughter of sexual impropriety, he will kill both the offending man and his own female relation. The relatives of those killed will not seek revenge if the killing was for sexual misconduct, and the killer will not be punished by the local *jirga*. Indeed, the killer's neighbors will praise him for upholding the honor of his family.

Another trait of the Pakhtuns is their deep belief in equality among men. Pakhtuns do not have chiefs. A *khan* or a *malik* is only a first among equals. Similarly, a Pakhtun servant is free to help himself to food at his master's table and to participate in dinner conversation.

In modern government, Pakhtun bureaucrats are far more accessible to ordinary people than are Punjabi or Sindhi officials. And if a Pakhtun businessman asks for tea, he will offer some to the employee who brings it to him, while a Punjabi or Sindhi employer will rarely do so.

The language the Pakhtuns speak is Pashto, a language related to Persian but incorporating the guttural pronunciations used in Arabic. Pashto also includes words from Sanskrit, Greek, and Pali, the language of ancient Buddhists.

Although Pakhtun warriors have passed down a rich heritage of Pashto poetry, few Pakhtuns today use Pashto when they are writing prose. Like Punjabis, when Pakhtuns learn to read and write, they usually do it in Urdu. Urdu may be less stirring than Pashto, but it has a much wider vocabulary.

Many Pakhtuns live beyond the boundaries of the North-West Frontier Province. Five hundred thousand ethnic Pakhtuns live in the Northern Areas, where they are a majority. These people speak Shina, a language similar to Pashto. In Karachi there are well over a million Pakhtuns, and almost 2 million Pakhtuns live in northeast Baluchistan. During the 1980's, over 700,000 refugees fled the war in Afghanistan to the safety of Baluchistan. Half of these refugees are Pakhtuns, so today there are almost as many Pakhtuns living in Baluchistan as there are Baluch. The Baluch worry that they may gradually lose control of their province to the industrious Pakhtuns.

The Baluch

The Baluch make up 3.5 percent of the population of Pakistan and also 2 percent of the population of Iran and Afghanistan. They are typically tall, with light-tan skin and dark-brown eyes.

Some Baluch live in oases and grow wheat, apples, and apricots. More often, Baluch are herders of sheep and goats. Nomads, they migrate as an extended family, or as a branch of a tribe, to wherever the desert sprouts enough vegetation for their animals to graze. They milk their goats and eat their sheep, and sell the hides and wool. Once or twice a year the men go to a large town and earn extra money as manual laborers.

Two women wearing burqas *at a tuberculosis prevention center in Rawalpindi.*
United Nations

Like the Pakhtuns, the Baluch follow a code of honor that calls for revenge, hospitality, and the punishment of illicit sex by death, although the Baluch are less likely to prolong a feud.

Unlike the Pakhtuns, the Baluch are not egalitarian. A Baluch tribe is headed by a *sardar*, and the *sardar*'s word is law. The Baluch bow low to their *sardar*, and are completely loyal to him. One Baluch man, when asked what he wanted for his tribe, replied, "Whatever our *sardar* tells us."

Many *sardar*s discourage education and block economic development. They do this to keep their authority safe from challenge; but their resistance to change is one of the main reasons the Baluch are the poorest and least educated people in Pakistan.

Most Baluch speak Baluchi, a language similar enough to Persian that the majority of Baluch can understand a Persian speaker. Because the Baluch have been nomads, their language was not written down in the Persian script until the twentieth century, and even now the vol-

The Shezan Bakery in Quetta, Baluchistan, is also a gun shop. Mark Weston

A young Baluch laborer.   United Nations

ume of written Baluchi is quite small. One fifth of the Baluch people speak Brahui, a Dravidian language that may derive from the language spoken in the ancient city of Mohenjodaro 4,500 years ago.

The Urdu Language

Urdu (pronounced OOR-doo) is the official language of Pakistan. Though only the Mohajirs speak Urdu as a native tongue, over 70 percent of Pakistan's people understand it, and in cities the number of people who understand some Urdu is probably over 95 percent. In 1947, the founders of Pakistan chose Urdu as the national language

Some Urdu Words and Phrases

Peace be unto you. (Hello.)	Salahm alaikum.
And on you be peace.	Vahlaikum us-salahm.
How are you?	Ahp kaise hain?
What is your name?	Ahp kah nahm kyah hai?
Good morning. Good evening.	Subah ba-khair. Shahm ba-khair.
Thank you.	Shukriyah.
God willing.	Insha'allah.
Good-bye.	Khudah hahfeez.
Sir or Ma'am	Jee.
Yes. No.	Hahn. Naheen.
I do not speak Urdu.	Mujhe oordoo naheen ahtee.
Do you speak English?	Kyah ahp ko angrezee ahtee hai?
Good; bad; enough.	Achah; kharahb; bas.
How much is it?	Yih kitnee keemat kah hai?
Where is _____?	_____ ka-hahn hai?
I, You	Main, Ahp (or Tum, the familiar)
1, 2, 3, 4, 5	ek, do, teen, chahr, pahnch
6, 7, 8, 9, 10	cheh, saht, ahth, nau, das
20, 30, 40, 50	bees, tees, chalees, pa-chahs
100	ek sau

because it was geographically neutral. Urdu was the refined language that educated Muslims (and many Hindus) had used for centuries throughout the subcontinent. Its use by government officials, therefore, could not make one region of Pakistan dominant over another.

As a spoken language, Urdu is almost identical to Hindi, the language of northern India. The grammar and basic words are the same. The difference between the two languages is that in Hindi many of the more complex words come from Sanskrit, while in Urdu many of these words come from Persian or Arabic.

Written Hindi and written Urdu, however, use completely different alphabets. Hindi is written in the left-to-right Devanagari script of ancient India. Urdu is written in a slightly modified Persian script that was brought to India by Persian-speaking conquerors. The Urdu script is almost the same as Arabic, and like Arabic is written from right to left. Its alphabet, however, is slightly different.

Since 1947, Urdu has been the main language that teachers use in Pakistan's public schools. Urdu is also the main language of television and radio broadcasts, so throughout Pakistan Urdu is widely understood today by rich and poor alike. It has become a national language in reality as well as by decree.

In the cities of the Punjab, it is common for children to speak Urdu at home even when their parents speak Punjabi. The parents and children understand each other because Urdu and Punjabi are similar in grammar, vocabulary, and pronunciation, rather like Italian and Spanish.

Saraiki

In the southern Punjab, from the city of Multan to the northernmost edge of Sind, people speak a language called Saraiki. The Saraiki language is a hybrid of Punjabi and Sindhi, but contains some Baluchi words too. Approximately 15 percent of the Punjab's people speak Saraiki, about one out of every ten Pakistanis.

English

The best educated and most prosperous people in Pakistan speak English as well as they speak their native language. Often they switch from one language to the other in mid sentence. Their children, perhaps 2 or 3 percent of children nationwide, start studying English at age five or six, usually in private schools where only English is spoken.

Pakistanis in public schools also study English, but it is only one course among many, and the quality of instruction is poor. In the largest cities, even illiterate Pakistanis often speak several dozen words of English.

English is vital for any Pakistani who wishes to get ahead. It is the language used in university classrooms, army manuals, technical training, business with foreign nations, and in American movies. Pakistan's legal system is based on British common law, so lawsuits above the village level are often tried in English. Legal contracts and government documents are also commonly written in English.

A knowledge of English is such an important ingredient for success in Pakistan that a middle-class family will make almost any sacrifice to save enough money to send at least one son to an English-speaking school.

Early History
(2500 B.C.–A.D. 1526)

The Indus Civilization

In 1922, along the Indus River about 200 miles (320 kilometers) from the sea, an archeologist named Rakhal Das Banerji dug into a series of mounds that the local people called Mohenjodaro, which in Sindhi means "Mound of the Dead." There, to his astonishment, Banerji found the ruins of a large city built 4,500 years ago by a long-forgotten civilization. Archeologists also discovered a second ancient city 400 miles (640 kilometers) upstream, near the Ravi River in the Punjab, close to the modern town of Harappa.

Since then, archeologists have found seventy ancient cities and towns along the Indus River and its tributaries—an expanse hundreds of miles wide, and far larger than the Fertile Crescent in Mesopotamia. Mohenjodaro and Harappa were the largest of these cities; each was once home to between twenty and fifty thousand people. The two cities were built quite suddenly, around 2500 B.C. They were well planned, built with standardized bricks and having wide streets running north to south and east to west.

Perhaps the idea of irrigating fields and living in cities, which first began in Turkey and Mesopotamia, had finally reached the Indus valley. But the Indus River civilization was not a colony of Mesopotamia, for its crops, writing, art, and architecture were fundamentally different from those of the Middle East.

Archeologists say that the cities of the Indus flourished for a thousand years, from 2500 to 1500 B.C. Surrounding these cities were irrigated fields, where short, dark-skinned people grew wheat, barley, peas, sesame, melons, and cotton. The people of the Indus were the first on earth to grow cotton, and the first to spin it into thread and weave it into cloth. There were also kilns in the fields, belching thick smoke as craftsmen made pottery and baked tens of thousands of bricks, all the same size and shape.

At the western edge of Mohenjodaro, according to archeologists who have studied the city, was a fortress on a hill, with walls of burned brick forty to fifty feet high. Inside was a central granary built of brick and timber, where kernels of wheat and barley were kept dry and well ventilated. A few yards away, brick steps led down to a long bathing pool, where priests conducted a ritual of cleansing and purification.

From the fortress, Mohenjodaro stretched all the way to the Indus River, a mile to the east. In the streets, men wore thin robes and left their right shoulders bare. They put their hair in buns in the back and kept their beards trim. The women wore very short skirts, and nothing from the waist up except for a number of necklaces and earrings made of stone and clay beads. Wealthy women, however, wore fan-shaped headdresses and necklaces of jade, silver, and gold.

The unpaved, thirty-foot-wide streets of Mohenjodaro were laid out

Important Dates in Pakistan's Early History

2500 B.C.	Indus civilization begins
1500 B.C.	Aryans conquer India, form the Hindu religion
326 B.C.	Alexander the Great enters the Punjab
3rd century B.C.	Taxila becomes a city of Buddhist learning
A.D. 320	Gupta dynasty begins a golden age of Hindu culture
A.D. 711	Arabs conquer Sind, bringing Islam to India
A.D. 1021	Mahmud of Ghazni conquers the Punjab and makes Lahore its capital
A.D. 1206	Qutb-ud-din Aibak begins the Sultanate of Delhi
14th century	Sultanate's soldiers gradually form the Urdu language
1526	Sultanate of Delhi ends; Mughal Empire begins

at right angles, making huge rectangular blocks over three hundred yards long. In the middle of these streets were drains carrying waste out of the city. They were covered by brick, but there were manholes to allow access and repair. Many houses had earthenware chutes that carried waste from indoor seat toilets out to drains in the streets—a sanitary system unequaled until well into the nineteenth century.

Along the sides of Mohenjodaro's wide streets there were only walls with no windows. The real life of the city, archeologists say, was not on

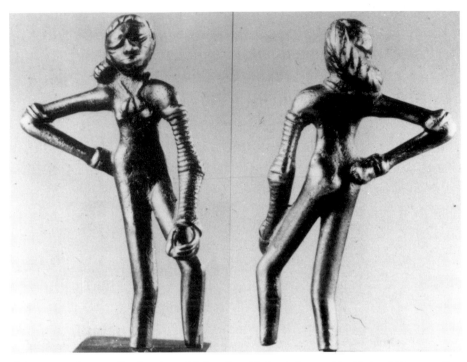

A bronze sculpture of a dancing girl found at Mohenjodaro. The National Museum, New Delhi

the wide streets, but in the smaller lanes and alleys. There, merchants built shops two stories high, sold food, pottery, and cloth, and used standardized weights and measures. Blacksmiths forged copper and tin into bronze and made knives, axes, plates, and cups. Some blacksmiths also made bronze animals, such as the humped zebu bull, which seems to have been both a farm animal and an object of worship.

Many homes were also two stories high, with staircases and brick walls. Inside, each house faced an interior courtyard, an arrangement common in Pakistan even today. There, children played with earthenware rattles, marbles, whistles, bulls, and toy carts.

On the banks of the Indus, barges full of grain arrived from smaller towns. Occasionally, archeologists speculate, there was a large ship with a single square sail, with porters loading a cargo of cotton cloth, gold, silver, incense, ivory, monkeys, and peacocks, as they prepared the ship for its long journey to the distant cities of Mesopotamia.

Archeologists who have studied the Indus civilization agree that it was a surprisingly uniform and unchanging society. The layout of streets, the style of brick, the designs on pottery, and the statues of bulls remained the same not only from one town to the next, but also from one century to the next.

The reason for this uniformity is unknown, for no one has yet deciphered the Indus script. Archeologists have identified about four hundred pictographic characters, but they have never found a seal or a piece of pottery with more than seventeen of them together. It is possible that the characters are just proper names.

Stone seals from Mohenjodaro.   George F. Dales and the University Museum, Philadelphia

Deforestation

Sometime around 1700 B.C., the cities of the Indus began to deteriorate. Houses were subdivided, drainpipes fell into disrepair, and pottery became cruder. Probably crops failed repeatedly, driving thousands of refugees into already crowded cities. Perhaps an earthquake or a shift in natural cycles caused the Indus to change its course, but it is equally likely that crop declines were indirectly caused by human beings.

The people of the Indus baked their bricks to ensure that the walls of their buildings were weatherproof. The fires in the kilns that baked these millions of bricks consumed an enormous amount of fuel, and workers chopped down whole forests to stoke these fires. Over time, more and more of the surface of the Indus valley was exposed to Pakistan's blazing subtropical sun. This may have caused the soil to erode, which in turn may have led to a change in the course of the Indus. Either of these conditions would have caused crop failures.

Stone seals found throughout Mohenjodaro and Harappa show animals such as rhinoceroses, tigers, and bears—clearly indicating that once there was jungle or marshland near the Indus. But by 1700 B.C., the Indus Valley may already have begun to resemble the semidesert that it is today.

The Aryans

Around 1500 B.C., the Indus civilization suddenly ended forever. Tall, fair-skinned people from southern Russia who called themselves Aryans ("kinsmen") rode in on horseback, destroyed the cities of the Indus, and enslaved their people.

The warlike Aryans knew nothing about city life. They lived in wooden huts in small villages and counted their wealth in cattle. But

Indo-European Languages

The language of the Aryans, an early form of Sanskrit, is the root of all the chief languages of Pakistan: Punjabi, Urdu, Sindhi, Pashto, and Baluchi. It is also the root of Hindi and Bengali, the main languages of northern India and Bangladesh. In addition, this early Sanskrit is a primary root of Persian, Greek, Russian, Gaelic, Latin, and German, and thus also English. When the Aryans left their home in southern Russia sometime around 2000 B.C., they migrated not only to India, but also to Iran, which is named after the Aryans, and even as far west as Ireland (Erin), which is also named for the Aryans. To this day, basic words like "mother" and "father" are virtually the same in all of these "Indo-European" languages. When the Aryans conquered India 3,500 years ago, they called their parents "mata" and "pitar."

their hymns, the "Vedas," marked the beginning of the Hindu religion, which spread all across India during the thousand years of Aryan rule. The Aryans also began Hinduism's rigid caste system, dividing the people of the subcontinent into five broad groups: Brahmins (priests), Kshatriyas (warriors), Vaishyas (farmers, craftsmen, and traders), Shudras (menial workers) and Panchamas (outcasts, more commonly known as "Untouchables").

Greeks, Buddhists, Guptas, and Huns

By 500 B.C., Aryan India had divided into many small kingdoms. During the next 1,200 years, many groups gained and lost power, but few had any lasting effect on modern-day Pakistan. In villages, the people of the farming caste continued to grow grain, often collectively. They usually paid one fourth of their crops to their rulers as taxes, and smaller amounts for the services of local craftsmen and priests.

In 326 B.C., the Greek conqueror Alexander the Great led 25,000 soldiers from Afghanistan into the Punjab, but he stayed only a year and a half before his homesick men demanded to return to the west. Around 175 B.C., however, some of the descendents of these soldiers conquered the Punjab once more. These Asiatic Greeks, called Bactrians, introduced India to the solar calendar, the seven-day week, and the hour.

One of the cities they conquered, Taxila, near modern Islamabad, had become a great center of Buddhist art and knowledge during the reign of a Buddhist king named Asoka in the third century B.C. Buddhism, like Hinduism, is a religion that accepts many gods as well as a

Ruins of the ancient Buddhist city of Thakht-i-Bhai in the North-West Frontier Province.   Diana Saint James

belief in reincarnation. Many Greeks, including the Bactrian King Menander, converted to Buddhism, as did many low-caste Hindus in the Punjab and Sind.

From A.D. 320 to 500, the Gupta dynasty united all of northern India under Hindu rule. Because India's spices and cotton cloth were in demand around the world, it was a time of prosperity and a golden age for Hindu science and culture. But around A.D. 500, fierce Huns galloped in from western Siberia. They overthrew the Guptas and completely destroyed the Greek Buddhist city of Taxila, beginning a new era of political fragmentation. For two hundred years, India was again divided into small Hindu kingdoms.

The Arrival of Islam

In 711, an Arab army brought to India a new religion, Islam, with a belief in just one God. Seventeen-year-old Muhammad bin Qasim, nephew of Hajjaj, ruler of Iraq and Persia, led an army of 12,000 men and 6,000 horses across Baluchistan and into Sind to avenge an act of piracy. With arrows of burning cotton, and a stone-throwing catapult that Arab soldiers lovingly called "the bride," Qasim and his fellow Muslims—followers of Islam—conquered Sind and joined it to the vast Arab empire that stretched westward all the way to Spain.

For three hundred years Sind was the only part of India under Muslim rule, but during this time tens of thousands of Buddhists and low-caste Hindus converted to Islam. They combined Arabic words with their own language, an early form of Hindi, to form a new language called Sindhi. The Muslim converts of Sind introduced the Arabs to advances in medicine, the use of the zero, the sine, decimals, and the so-called "Arabic" numerals that we all use today.

In 997, an Afghan warrior named Mahmud of Ghazni led thousands

Conversions to Islam

From the twelfth century onward millions of Hindus responded to the Muslim creed that all men and women are equal in the sight of God, and freely converted to Islam. Before long, Indian-born Muslims heavily outnumbered their Afghan rulers. Some Hindus converted to avoid the *jizya*, the tax on non-Muslims. Others sought promotion in a Muslim-ruled empire.

Most of the many Hindus who converted to Islam did so to escape their status as Untouchables or as members of the Shudra (menial-worker) caste. This was especially true in Bengal, where caste discrimination was severe, and where wandering Muslim saints of the Sufi sect converted whole villages of Hindus with the message that "lamps are different, but the light is the same." Low-caste peasants also converted to Islam in the Punjab, where Muslims had ruled continuously since the 1020's. In both of these densely populated provinces the Muslims eventually became the majority—and it was the existence of these majorities that eventually led to the creation of Pakistan.

of Muslim archers on horseback across the Khyber Pass in the first of seventeen raids of plunder deep into India. For thirty years Mahmud smashed and looted hundreds of Hindu and Buddhist temples, which he regarded as monuments to idols and abominations in the sight of God. He destroyed the armies of Hindu princes and raided their palaces, and his men took as much gold and jewelry and as many slaves as they could manage.

Although Mahmud was primarily interested in plunder, he added the Punjab and Sind to his empire, and in 1021 he made Lahore the Punjab's capital city. All the territory of what is now Pakistan was under Muslim rule, and it would remain so for eight hundred years.

Mahmud died in 1030, and for 150 years the Afghans left India in peace. But in 1179 Muhammad of Ghur led a new Afghan army across the Khyber Pass, and he was interested not only in plunder, but also in conquest. The invention of iron stirrups enabled his men to fire cross-bows in the midst of a gallop, and by 1203 they had conquered the Punjab, Sind, and the whole of northern India.

To commemorate his conquest, Muhammad of Ghur ordered the construction of the Mosque of the Might of Islam in the city of Delhi in 1200. This immense mosque, which includes a 240-foot-high minaret, was built on the site of a demolished Hindu temple, with stones from twenty-seven other Hindu shrines. One can only imagine the rage that Hindus must have felt at this time.

The Sultanate of Delhi

When Muhammad of Ghur died in 1206, General Qutb-ud-din Aibak broke away from his Afghan homeland and established a new, independent kingdom: the Sultanate of Delhi. Thirty-five sultans ruled this rich and powerful kingdom between 1206 and 1526, but the average reign of a sultan was only nine years because nineteen of them were assassinated. Most of the sultans were uneducated and cruel, and some persecuted Buddhists so relentlessly that the Buddhists fled to Nepal and Tibet, never to return to India.

One sultan was a woman, Razia Sultana, who ruled India from 1236 to 1240. She dressed like a man and stopped wearing a veil, but when she appointed a slave to be master of the royal stables, the nobles rebelled and put her younger brother on the throne.

In the 1250's, a Mongol warrior named Hulagu led his ferocious horsemen through the Middle East and massacred entire cities, including Baghdad and its 600,000 men, women, and children. (See *The Land and People of Mongolia*.) Refugees from all over the Islamic world streamed east into India, among them scholars, poets, physicians, and craftsmen. Overnight they transformed the cities of Delhi and Lahore into lively centers of Muslim art and culture.

Islam was in India to stay. Even the Hindi language, which ordinary soldiers spoke, borrowed so many words from Persian and Turkish, the languages used by officers, that by the year 1400 a new language emerged: Urdu, which is now the national language of Pakistan. Indeed, the name Urdu is Turkish for "of the camp."

From the mid-1300's onward, the sultans of Delhi organized their empire along feudal lines. Most sultans gave land grants or *jagir*s to their generals, who then had to provide a specified number of soldiers whenever the sultan needed them. In return, the generals collected the taxes on the sultans' land—usually one fourth of each peasant family's crop. As long as the peasants paid their taxes, the government left them alone.

It was an unfortunate system, because land returned to the sultan when a general died. There was no incentive for a general to improve his land or to loan money to a business. Instead, a commander would spend his money on luxuries while the money was still his to spend. This *jagir* system continued until the time of the British, and it is one reason why India never developed the kind of investment economy that enabled England and Japan to industrialize so rapidly.

The Mughal Empire (1526–1858)

The Mughal Empire was the golden age of India's Muslims. The vastness of its conquests, the luxury of its court life, and the grandeur of the architecture remain a source of deep pride for the people of Pakistan. The most famous monument of this era, the Taj Mahal, lies in India, not Pakistan, but Pakistanis take pleasure in the fact that the symbol of India, a nation 83 percent Hindu, is a Muslim tomb built for a beautiful Mughal queen.

The Mughal era was also the last time that Muslims held power before the creation of Pakistan in 1947, so when Pakistanis look to the past, they look to the Mughals. They remember especially the six Great Mughals who ruled between 1526 and 1707: Babur, Humayun, Akbar, Jahangir, Shah Jahan, and Aurangzeb. Some Pakistanis today still enjoy discussing which one of them was the best emperor.

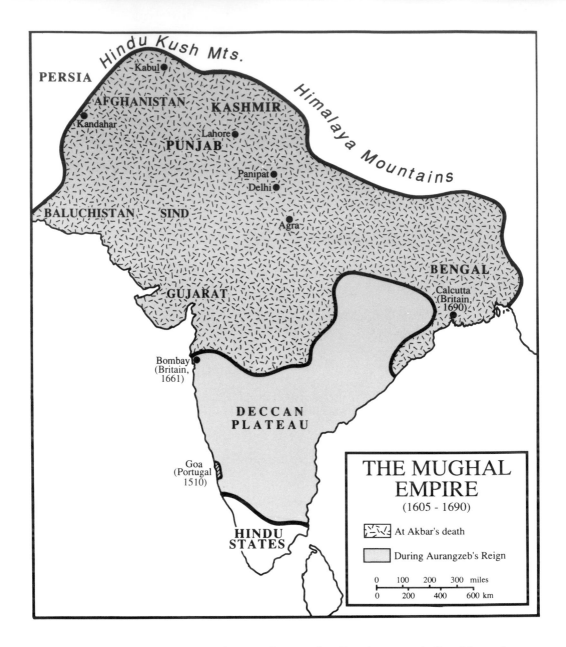

THE MUGHAL
EMPIRE
(1605 - 1690)

At Akbar's death

During Aurangzeb's Reign

| 0 | 100 | 200 | 300 miles |
| 0 | 200 | 400 | 600 km |

Mughal—often spelled Mogul—is the Persian word for Mongol. Babur, the first Mughal emperor, was a distant descendent of Genghis Khan on his mother's side, and of Timur (also known as Tamerlane), an equally fierce conqueror, on his father's side. The descendents of

· 54 ·

Timur were able warriors, but they were also educated men who enjoyed the Islamic culture of Persia. They kept their swords sharp, but they enjoyed poetry.

Babur

Babur was born in 1483 in a small kingdom called Fergana, which today is in Uzbekistan, north of Afghanistan. When his father died in 1494, Babur became king at the age of eleven. While still a teenager, he lost most of his kingdom to a nomadic tribe called the Uzbeks, but in 1504 he conquered Kabul, on the other side of the Hindu Kush, and made that Afghan city his new home. Several years later, he traded with the Turks and bought guns and cannons, new inventions at the time.

The Uzbeks' grip on his old kingdom was permanent, so Babur looked to a much richer prize: India. In the 1520's the Sultanate of Delhi was weakened by internal quarrels. Babur seized the opportunity presented by this weakness and led his army through the Khyber Pass, conquering the Punjab early in 1526.

The decisive battle against Sultan Ibrahim took place at Panipat, north of Delhi, on April 20, 1526. Babur led 25,000 well-disciplined men. Ibrahim had an army of 100,000 men, with 1,000 fighting elephants trained since birth to crush anything in their path. Unfortunately for the Sultan, the elephants had never heard cannon fire before, and they panicked during the battle. Babur's army killed 20,000 men that day, including Sultan Ibrahim himself.

Three days later, Babur's men seized the Sultan's treasury in the city of Agra. Babur calculated that one jewel, a massive diamond called the Koh-i-Nur (Mountain of Light), could buy enough grain to feed the entire world for three days. He gave it to his seventeen-year-old son

Humayun, who had fought bravely in battle. A few days later Babur proclaimed himself Emperor of India, and within three years he was indeed the master of most of northern India.

Throughout his life Babur kept a diary. It contained a forty-page description of the Hindu religion, Hindu numerals, and much of the animal and plant life of India. His memoir strongly influenced his immediate descendents, who learned from him to be tolerant of Hinduism and to delight in gardens and nature.

Humayun

When Babur died in 1530, his son Humayun became Emperor at age twenty-two. Humayun was highly superstitious, letting astrology dictate the decisions he made, the verdicts he issued, and even the clothes he wore. After ten years of misrule, his badly led army could no longer defend itself. An Afghan warrior from Bengal province named Sher Shah Sur conquered Delhi, crowned himself Emperor, and pursued Humayun.

Humayun rushed to the city of Agra, emptied the treasury, loaded his horses with jewels and gold, and fled for his life. With only a small army, Humayun at first wandered through the desert of Sind and then headed for Persia in hopes of raising a large army there. Along the way the dethroned Emperor once had nothing to eat but horsemeat boiled in a helmet.

In the desert Humayun fell in love with a fourteen-year-old girl named Hamida. A month passed before Hamida agreed to marry her thirty-three-year old Emperor, for in the desert in 1541 Humayun did not seem like much of a catch. Yet their child, Akbar, Humayun's first son, became one of the greatest rulers in India's history.

When Humayun finally arrived in Persia in 1544, the Shah of Persia supplied Humayun with soldiers, weapons, horses, and grain. In return, Humayun gave the Shah the enormous Koh-i-Nur diamond.

During his stay in Persia, Humayun admired the miniature paintings of two artists, Khwaja Abdus Samad and Mir Sayyid Ali. He invited them to come to Delhi once he reclaimed his throne. They did, and soon painters all over India copied their delicate, precise miniature style.

With his new army Humayun conquered Afghanistan in 1545. But he did not attack India until 1555, when his enemies, Sher Shah Sur and his son, were dead and the subcontinent was in anarchy. As Humayun's army swept through India, Humayun reclaimed the throne he had lost. But the unlucky emperor did not rule long. On January 24, 1556, Humayun fell down a flight of stairs, struck his head, and died. His thirteen-year-old son, Akbar, inherited an empire that was only six months old.

Akbar

It is fitting that in Arabic the name Akbar means "great," for Akbar is considered by many to be the greatest of the Mughal emperors. He ruled India for half a century, from 1556 to 1605, almost exactly the same years that Queen Elizabeth I ruled England. During his long reign he brought most of India under Mughal rule and made the subcontinent a freer, more prosperous, and more cultured place in which to live.

As a boy, Akbar learned how to fight with a bow and arrow, a lance, and a sword, and he learned how to assemble, load, and fire a gun. He also rode galloping horses and charging elephants. Because Akbar grew up in an army camp in Afghanistan rather than in a palace in India, he was the only Mughal emperor who never learned to read and write. Smooth-voiced servants read books and reports to him, and he held serious discussions daily with the most brilliant men in India.

During the first years of his reign, Akbar put down three rebellions. Later, Akbar waged war to extend his empire, conquering Bengal in 1575 and Kashmir in 1586.

In peacetime, one of Akbar's favorite ways to keep his army in shape was to hunt. On a royal hunt thousands of soldiers would form a huge circle and beat pans with sticks, scaring stags, antelopes, and sometimes even tigers into a center penned in by screens. The emperor would then hunt in a small area. During one hunt in 1567, 50,000 soldiers formed a circle 60 miles (100 kilometers) in diameter before moving inward. On another hunt in 1596, Akbar grabbed a stag by its horns but was knocked down and gored. It took him two months to heal.

Akbar hunted all over India. It helped him keep in touch with the people. During one hunt Akbar saw Hindus pay a "pilgrim tax" before they could worship at a shrine. Akbar abolished the tax.

Akbar also abolished the much-hated *jizya* in 1564. This was the tax that non-Muslims paid in return for Muslim protection. By this one act Akbar won the undying gratitude of the two thirds of the Indian people who were Hindu. The emperor further unified India by recruiting Hindus into the civil service and the higher ranks of the army.

Akbar also married Hindu princesses. He allowed them to continue to worship as Hindus inside his harem and even to put on Hindu festivals at court. These marriages cemented alliances with the Hindu princes called Rajputs. The armies of the Rajputs were not large enough to defeat the Mughals, but in their hilltop fortresses they could be dangerous enemies. Akbar let the Rajputs govern their own dominions; in return they recognized Mughal supremacy.

One of Akbar's closest advisers, Abul Fazl, wrote a 2,500-page history of Akbar's reign, illustrated with beautiful miniature paintings of battles, hunts, court life, and royal ceremonies. Akbar supported many scholars and painters, as well as architects, musicians, poets, and craftsmen.

Akbar's revenues were high because India was prosperous. Cotton and spices sold for good prices throughout Asia, and grain surpluses were common in an era with fewer people to feed than there are today. Peasants paid one third of their harvest in taxes, but no taxes at all when crops were poor.

As Akbar grew old, he became more of a religious freethinker. He talked with Hindu, Muslim, Sikh, Buddhist, and even Jesuit priests and asked them difficult questions, including some about Jesus, asking, for instance, why he didn't just get down from the cross. Akbar also ordered the translation of Hindu scriptures into Persian, so Muslims could read them.

Eventually Akbar formed his own religion, the Religion of God. He, Akbar, would be the arbiter of religious disputes. Orthodox Muslims were appalled. When Akbar died of internal bleeding on October 15, 1605, his Religion of God died too.

Jahangir

Akbar's eldest son, Salim, became Emperor at age thirty-six and took a new name, Jahangir (Seizer of the World).

The pleasure-loving Jahangir lived a life in which there was no limit to luxury. Meals, for example, consisted of up to fifty courses, including sherbet made from ice carried down from the Himalayas, served on plates of jade and gold.

Outdoors there were beautiful gardens. Spring water rushed up fountains, around pavilions, and down waterfalls. Mica (a wafer-thin crystal) was scattered on the ground to reflect the moonlight, and flowers such as jasmine and narcissi gave fragrance at night.

Indoors, young boys kept the palaces cool by pulling rope fans all day, and harems contained hundreds of women. In the end, Jahangir devoted himself to just one woman, but he did not meet her until he was forty-two and already had several children.

Jahangir married Mehrunissa in 1611 and renamed her Nur Jahan (Light of the World). Persian by descent, Nur Jahan was a widow: thirty-four years old, beautiful, brilliant, and ambitious. She set fashions by designing clothes, blending perfume, and writing poetry. She also shot tigers from an enclosed *howdah* on top of an elephant. Only her gun could be seen by men.

While Jahangir drank wine and smoked opium daily, Nur Jahan became the power behind the throne. Her relatives became top officials, and her niece, the beautiful Arjumand Banu, married Jahangir's eldest son, Khurram.

After Khurram won several victories against Hindu rebels, Jahangir was so pleased with his son that he renamed him Shah Jahan (Sovereign of the World). But in 1624, Jahangir ordered his son to go to Kandahar, in faraway Afghanistan. Shah Jahan refused. He would not travel so far from court when his father, who was ill, could die at any time and his brother Shahriyar might take the throne.

An angry Jahangir sent an army after his disobedient son, and it pursued Shah Jahan across India for three years. The chase ended on October 28, 1627, when, after a fairly calm reign of twenty-two years, Jahangir died.

Shah Jahan and the Taj Mahal

Shah Jahan had to fight for his throne. His brother Shahriyar raised an army, but the soldiers were inexperienced, and Shah Jahan defeated them easily in January 1628. His men then executed Shahriyar, along with another brother, two nephews, and two cousins. Their deaths insured that no one could challenge Shah Jahan's throne, but they also began a disastrous new pattern of family murder that would occur each time an emperor died.

Nur Jahan retired to the city of Lahore, where she built a tomb for Jahangir and designed another one for herself. Her niece, Arjumand Banu, was the new Queen of India. Shah Jahan gave his wife a new name: Mumtaz Mahal (Chosen One of the Palace).

Shah Jahan was completely devoted to Mumtaz Mahal. She did not dominate him the way Nur Jahan had dominated Jahangir, but she was clearly Shah Jahan's great love, best friend, and chief adviser. She read state documents and affixed the royal seal.

Mumtaz reigned as queen for only three and a half years before she died while giving birth to her fourteenth child in 1631. Shah Jahan was grief-stricken. For two years he wore simple clothes, ate plain food, and prohibited music at court.

Shah Jahan commissioned his finest architects to build for his wife a tomb "as beautiful as she was beautiful." The architects brought several wooden models of the Taj Mahal to the grieving emperor, who added his own suggestions. Then 20,000 craftsmen and laborers worked in the city of Agra for sixteen years to build the swelling dome, slender minarets, arched alcoves, and inlaid jewels of "the dream in marble," the Taj Mahal.

Shah Jahan also built the Shalimar Gardens in Lahore around 1640. With their fountains, waterfalls, and marble pavilions, these gardens are enjoyed today by millions of Pakistanis.

When Shah Jahan held a public audience in Delhi, he sat on the Peacock Throne. This jewel-studded chair lay underneath a canopy supported by twelve emerald pillars, topped by two golden peacocks whose tails were filled with diamonds, rubies, and pearls.

A miniature painting (14⅛ inches by 9¾ inches) of the Mughal emperor Shah Jahan on horseback. The Metropolitan Museum of Art, Gift of Alexander Smith Cochran (13.228.43)

Important Dates of the Mughal Empire

1526	Babur conquers most of northern India
1540–1555	Humayun loses and regains his throne
1556–1605	Reign of Akbar
1564	Akbar abolishes the *jizya*, the tax on non-Muslims
1632–1648	Construction of the Taj Mahal during the reign of Shah Jahan
1658–1707	Reign of Aurangzeb
1679	Aurangzeb reimposes the *jizya*
1739	Persia's Nadir Shah invades Delhi, marking the end of Mughal power
1857–1858	Executions by the British following the Rebellion of 1857 end the Mughal Dynasty; Bahadur Shah II exiled to Burma

To pay for Shah Jahan's lavish spending, peasants paid higher taxes, even when harvests were poor. Many peasants hid what few belongings they had, or left their farms altogether to try their luck in the city.

Shah Jahan's eldest son, Dara Shikoh, was a scholarly gentleman who spent much of his time translating the Hindu *Upanishads* into Persian. But while Dara was enjoying the contemplative life at court, his younger brother, Aurangzeb, spent twelve years fighting Hindu warriors in the Deccan, the rugged hills of south central India. An orthodox Muslim, Aurangzeb spent more time in prayer than in his harem. And he despised Dara for his interest in Hinduism, calling him his "Disgraceful Brother."

In September 1657 a kidney blockage prevented Shah Jahan from urinating for three days. Aurangzeb, wanting to be at court if his father died, brought his army north, near Agra. Shah Jahan recovered quickly, but the events of succession were already in motion. Aurangzeb routed his brother's inexperienced army. Then he surrounded Agra's Red Fort and cut off its water supply, forcing his father, Shah Jahan, to surrender to him on June 4, 1658.

Aurangzeb

Aurangzeb proclaimed himself emperor on July 21, 1658, explaining that it was necessary because Shah Jahan had allowed the "infidel" Dara Shikoh to spread Hinduism, the religion of idols. The new emperor confined his father to the Red Fort in Agra. For eight years the dethroned king read works of Persian literature and stared often at his beloved wife's mausoleum, the Taj Mahal, until he died in 1666.

After Dara was captured, Aurangzeb paraded his brother in tattered clothes through the streets of Delhi before beheading him. Meanwhile, Aurangzeb's oldest son, Muhammad Sultan, tried to rescue his grandfather, Shah Jahan. But Aurangzeb captured him quickly and threw him into prison. Thus Aurangzeb began his reign by imprisoning both his father and his son.

Aurangzeb ruled India for forty-nine years. To non-Muslims his reign seems disastrous, for although he extended the territory of the Mughal empire, he spent so much money on war that the weakened empire crumbled soon after his death. But to conservative Muslims, including many Pakistanis, Aurangzeb was the greatest of the Mughals because of his strict Muslim orthodoxy and his absolute refusal to be tolerant of Hinduism, with its caste system and its belief in many gods.

In 1668 Aurangzeb outlawed Hindu religious festivals. In 1679 he reimposed the *jizya*, the tax on non-Muslims, 115 years after Akbar had abolished it. When crowds of Hindus gathered in Agra to protest the tax, Aurangzeb ordered his soldiers to charge their elephants toward the protesters and trample them to death.

Aurangzeb's most extreme action against Hindus was to encourage his fellow Muslims to burn Hindu temples to the ground. Across India, Muslims destroyed thousands of Hindu shrines, many of them centuries old.

Never again would Muslims and Hindus work together with the degree of harmony they had enjoyed under Akbar. The hatred Aurangzeb unleashed was too great, the gulf between Hinduism and Islam too wide. Unlike Europe's Protestants and Catholics, who also fought in the seventeenth century but who gradually grew more tolerant of each other, India's Hindus and Muslims grew further apart. They worshipped different gods, recited different scriptures, and over the centuries came to honor different prophets and saints.

In 1681, Aurangzeb marched south to the hills of the Deccan Plateau in order to extend his empire's southern frontier. He stayed and fought Hindu armies for twenty-six years. When Aurangzeb moved, 170,000 soldiers and 300,000 civilians followed. They lived in tent cities nine miles wide that included 250 bazaars, 30,000 elephants, and 100,000 pack animals—a "walking kingdom." Wherever the royal camp moved, the tents were pitched in exactly the same arrangement as before.

Aurangzeb did capture some territory from the Hindu "mountain rats," as he called them, but the cost to the empire was enormous. Tens of thousands of Mughal soldiers lost their lives, and billions of rupees were wasted while Aurangzeb spent years taking one insignificant hill fort after another. Aurangzeb continued his soldier's life even into his eighties, feared by all and loved by none. One of his daughters, Zeb-un-Nissa, wrote:

O waterfall! Why are you weeping?
In whose sorrowful memory have you wrinkled your brow?
What is the pain that impelled you, like myself, the whole night,
To strike your head against stone and cry?

By the end of his reign even Aurangzeb began to realize how much of the Mughal Empire's wealth and power he had squandered. At age eighty-eight he confessed to a son, "I do not know who I am nor what I have been doing. I have sinned terribly, and I know not to what punishment I shall be doomed."

Aurangzeb died a few days later, on February 20, 1707, during his morning prayers. After forty-nine years of puritanical Muslim rule, Hindus across India welcomed the news.

The Decline of the Empire

Aurangzeb was the last Mughal ruler to keep the empire strong. After his death, there was a civil war among his sons and nephews, and eight emperors reigned over the next fifty-two years. Gradually provinces such as Bengal to the east and Hyderabad to the south quit paying taxes and became independent of the Mughals in everything but name.

Delhi itself was invaded: first by Nadir Shah of Persia, who marched off with the Peacock Throne in 1739, and later by Hindu Marathas from central India, who stripped Mughal tombs and palaces of their precious metals in 1760.

The beneficiary of the vacuum of power in India was the British East India Company. Since 1690 the company had operated small trading posts in Bombay and Calcutta. But in the second half of the eighteenth century the East India Company financed a well-disciplined army that gradually won control of most of India. By 1803 the company even ruled much of Delhi, although it continued to defer to the Mughal emperor in order to minimize Muslim resentment. The once-mighty emperor now reigned over only the roughly two square miles (five square kilometers) of Delhi inside the walls of the city's Red Fort.

In Sind province, power passed to a group of local Muslim landowners called amirs, who taxed their tenant farmers heavily until the British annexed Sind in 1843.

In the Punjab, Sikh warriors led by Ranjit Singh formed a state of their own in the first decade of the 1800's. (The Sikhs, who speak Punjabi and whose men always wear turbans, combine the Muslim belief in one god with the Hindu belief in reincarnation.)

For forty years the Sikh kingdom in the Punjab was the only state left in India completely free from British influence. But shortly after Ranjit Singh died, the Sikhs started a war against the British in 1845 and were defeated in 1849. The British took over the Punjab and installed an unusually enlightened government there. They lowered taxes, promoted irrigation, and allowed full religious freedom. In just a few years the British won the Sikhs' full loyalty. This loyalty proved vital to them during the Rebellion of 1857.

The Rebellion of 1857 marked the end of the Mughal Dynasty. The revolt began when British officers taught their native Indian troops to bite the tip off a cartridge before loading it into a new kind of rifle. It is unknown whether the cartridge grease was made from beef fat, which is forbidden to Hindus, or pork fat, which is forbidden to Muslims. But enraged soldiers of both faiths turned on their British officers, killed them, and marched to Delhi.

In Delhi, the rebellious troops burst into the decaying palace of the Mughal emperor on May 11, 1857, and proclaimed the elderly Bahadur Shah II as the leader of their great revolt. But the rebellion took place only in Delhi and a few cities along the Ganges River, and it was

Miss Wheeler Defending Herself Against the Sepoys at Cawnpore. *British propaganda during the Rebellion of 1857. Sepoys were Indian soldiers in the British army.* The Bettmann Archive

largely confined to Muslims. All but a few Hindus were indifferent. Sikh soldiers stayed loyal to the British and helped them to retake Delhi and capture the royal family in September 1857. A young British captain then executed all nine of the Emperor's sons, ending the Mughal dynasty forever.

The following year a British court exiled Bahadur Shah II to Burma (also called Myanmar). Shortly before he died in 1862, the seventeenth and last Mughal emperor mourned,

All that I loved is gone, like a garden robbed of its beauty by autumn. I am only a memory of splendor.

CHAPTER VI

British Rule and the Rise of the Muslim League (1858–1946)

Modernization

It took a full year for British soldiers to put down the Rebellion of 1857. Once the fighting was over, the British government took control of India away from the East India Company and began to rule the subcontinent directly. Using the labor and taxes of the Indian people, the British supervised the building of railroads, irrigation canals, telegraph lines, post offices, sewers, hospitals, schools, and universities.

Railroads were the most dramatic improvement. Between 1853 and 1900, the British built 25,000 miles (40,000 kilometers) of tracks in every part of India, along with workshops to build and repair locomotives. Journeys that once had taken a month now took only a day. Across India, men, women, and children boarded train compartments (or sat on the roofs of boxcars) to visit friends, relatives, and holy shrines.

The spread of the railroads encouraged farmers to grow cash crops such as cotton, because crops could be easily sent now from farm to port. In the early nineteenth century, however, many of India's cotton-weaving workshops went bankrupt because of competition from the textile mills of England. The English factories produced cloth much more cheaply than was possible in India. But in the 1860's, during the U.S. Civil War, the supply of American cotton to England stopped. The price of cotton tripled, and farmers in the Punjab, Sind, and elsewhere

This 1988 photograph of soldiers in the Khyber Rifles Regiment in full dress shows the continuing British influence on the army of Pakistan. U.N. Photo 1564605/J. Isaac

planted hundreds of thousands of acres of cotton to meet the new worldwide demand.

As cotton planting expanded, wealthy Hindu businessmen built dozens of textile mills near Bombay. They were dangerous and dusty places to work, but at least Indians were making cloth again. By 1914, there were 264 mills producing cotton cloth in India, and only a small amount of raw cotton was sent to England.

Irrigation made it possible for farmers to plant so much cotton. Between 1850 and 1900, British engineers repaired canals, dug water wells in the desert, and made dry land fertile by irrigating 8 million acres in the Punjab and Sind alone.

The British also directed the laying of 20,000 miles (32,000 kilometers) of telegraph wire by 1880, although what really changed communications in India was the creation of a postal service. Thanks to the post office, an illiterate farmer could dictate a letter to a village scribe and send it to any town in India. The scribe could also receive newspapers from faraway cities.

The Muslims Become Powerless

Many Hindus learned English and took advantage of new opportunities. They started banks and businesses and became government officials. But most Muslims continued working as farmers and foot soldiers. This was partly because the British still distrusted Muslims in the aftermath of the 1857 rebellion and rarely appointed them to the civil service or to the officer corps of the army. But it was also because many Muslims still preferred to study their holy scripture, the Qur'an (also spelled Koran), rather than Western science or the English language. As late as the 1880's, only 4 percent of the students at Indian universities were Muslims, even though Muslims accounted for one fourth of India's population.

One man who changed the attitude of Muslims toward Western education was Syed Ahmad Khan. He argued that Muslims should not be threatened by modern science, for the Qur'an, the Word of God, could not be in conflict with nature, the Work of God. He founded the Mohammedan Anglo Oriental College in 1875, and slowly the number of Muslim students at all universities began to increase.

Still, Muslims frequently felt like aliens in their own land. Many Britons were racists, calling both Hindus and Muslims "wogs" or even "niggers." High-caste Hindus often regarded Muslims as impure and refused even to eat with them.

The Founding of the Muslim League

In 1906, a new British government planned elections for seats on councils that advised the Viceroy, the British colonial ruler. Everyone in India welcomed these elections, but some Muslims worried that Hindu politicians might win all the seats, because Hindus comprised almost three fourths of India's people.

To protect Muslim interests, seventy wealthy landowners and lawyers met in December 1906 and formed the All-India Muslim League, the organization that eventually led Pakistan to independence in 1947. The Muslim League asked the British to set aside a percentage of council seats for Muslims, and to hold separate elections for these seats so that Muslim voters could elect their own representatives.

Hindus objected, but the British government granted the Muslim League's request and held separate elections for Muslim seats in 1910. The British did this in part to be fair to Muslims, and in part because they wanted to keep the politicians of India divided. Whatever motive was stronger, the holding of separate elections for Muslims was a big step toward renewed Muslim power.

A Brief Hindu–Muslim Unity

One Muslim elected to the national council in 1910 was Muhammad Ali Jinnah, the man who founded Pakistan in 1947. Jinnah was a brilliant lawyer from Bombay who believed that Hindus and Muslims needed only to unite to win India's independence from Britain. He worked hard not only as a member of the Muslim League, but also as a member of the Congress Party, a primarily Hindu group of powerful lawyers and editors who believed that India should govern itself as a secular state.

In 1916, in the city of Lucknow, Jinnah met with the president of the Congress Party and negotiated the Lucknow Pact, an agreement between the Muslim League and the Congress Party. Under the agreement, the Muslim League supported the party's demand that Britain make India a self-governing dominion, like Canada or Australia. In return, the Congress Party agreed to the principle of separate legislative seats for Muslims, chosen in separate elections. Congress also promised that no bill affecting Muslims would ever become law if three fourths of Muslim legislators opposed it.

The Lucknow Pact soothed Muslim fears of Hindu domination and put Muslim support squarely behind Congress's demand of dominion status for India. It was a triumph for Jinnah, who as "the Ambassador of Hindu–Muslim unity" was clearly a potential prime minister once India became a self-governing dominion.

Muslim Disillusionment

Oddly enough, it was the great Mohandas Gandhi who unwittingly helped to end the Hindu–Muslim unity of the 1910's. When it became clear in 1920 that the British were not going to grant dominion status to India anytime soon, Gandhi began a campaign of boycotts and civil disobedience in protest. But Gandhi was not just a political leader, he was also a spiritual teacher. And although Gandhi had the deepest respect for Islam, many Muslims nevertheless saw his movement as fundamentally Hindu in character, and this made them uncomfortable.

Muhammad Ali Jinnah, for example, called Gandhi a "Hindu revivalist," and thought his civil disobedience campaign would lead only to chaos. At a Congress Party meeting in December 1920, Jinnah was booed off the stage for referring to the Hindu leader as "*Mr.* Gandhi" instead of as "Mahatma," which in Hindi means "great soul." Jinnah, who only three years earlier had been one of the most promising lead-

Citizens of Bombay flee the colonial police during a protest against the arrest of Gandhi in 1932. UPI/Bettmann

ers of the Congress Party, was now completely out of place in Gandhi's new movement. He quit the Congress Party in disgust, and from 1921 onward he devoted his energies to the Muslim League instead.

Although Jinnah and many other Muslims were alienated by the Congress Party, they still believed in Hindu–Muslim unity as the means to win self-government from the British. But even this desire for unity was shattered in 1928, when the Congress Party issued a report repudiating its past approval of separate elections for Muslim representatives.

The secular leaders of the Congress Party saw no reason why they could not represent Muslims as fairly and impartially as they would Hindus. Nevertheless, their report marked the end of Hindu–Muslim unity. Without separate elections, Jinnah and other Muslim leaders feared domination by a Hindu majority more than they feared the continuation of British rule.

The Demand for Pakistan

The idea of a separate Muslim nation in India began with the great Urdu poet Muhammad Iqbal. In a 1930 speech to the Muslim League, Iqbal offered his vision:

I would like to see the Punjab, the North-West Frontier Province, Sind and Baluchistan amalgamated into a single State. Self-government . . . [is] the final destiny of the Muslims.

Three years later, a college student named Chaudhry Rahmat Ali came up with a name for the Muslim nation: "Pakistan." In Urdu it means "Land of the Pure," but it is also an acronym: "P" is for Punjab, "A" for Afghania (a name Rahmat preferred to the North-West Frontier Province), "K" for Kashmir, an "I" that occurs in English but not in Urdu, "S" is for Sind, and "TAN" is for Baluchistan.

Muhammad Ali Jinnah, The Founder of Pakistan

Muhammad Ali Jinnah (1876–1948) is one of the two giants of modern Indian history. The other is Mohandas Gandhi. In the 1940's Jinnah united the subcontinent's 100 million Muslims behind his demand for a separate nation to be called "Pakistan." Under his leadership, the Muslims became so adamant that by 1947 the British could not leave India without first dividing it in two. Pakistan owes its very existence to Jinnah's drive and tenacity.

Jinnah, who in 1947 became Pakistan's first leader, is as highly honored in Pakistan as George Washington is in the United States. Nearly every Pakistani reveres him as the Quaid-i-Azam (Great Leader) who rescued Muslims from permanent domination by India's caste-conscious Hindus.

Most citizens of India, however, and some Western historians, have a very different view of Jinnah. They would have preferred a united India, stretching from Iran to Burma, with Hindus and Muslims living as neighbors and friends. They see Jinnah as the man who destroyed this possibility by stirring up so much religious passion that in the end the partition of India was the only alternative to civil war.

Could India have remained united, with its religious groups living together in harmony? Possibly, but in the 1940's most of the subcontinent's Muslims did not think so. They rallied behind Jinnah and demanded a nation of their own. Today, few people in Pakistan regret the partition.

Jinnah was born in 1876, the son of a rich hide merchant in Karachi. He studied law in London from 1893 to 1896 and then returned to India to practice law in Bombay. He earned a reputation for being honest, precise, and hardworking, and was soon rich enough to buy a mansion by the sea.

Handsome, very cool and reserved, and always wearing a monocle and a business suit, Jinnah was not a devout Muslim. He ate pork, drank alcohol, and rarely prayed at a mosque. At the age of forty-one he married a non-Muslim, a lively eighteen-year-old girl of the Parsi faith named Ruttenbai Petit.

Jinnah began his career working for Hindu–Muslim unity. But as Mohandas Gandhi's followers grew in number, Jinnah and other members of the Muslim League felt increasingly alienated from a movement that to them seemed spiritual rather than political. Jinnah quit the dominant Congress Party in 1921. His marriage also soured. The austere, disciplined Jinnah had too little in common with his vivacious wife. In 1928 Ruttenbai Petit left him; she died just one year later of a drug overdose.

Disillusioned politically and emotionally, Jinnah left India in 1929 to practice law in London. The Muslim League grew very weak in his absence, and his friends begged him to come home.

In 1935 Jinnah returned to India to reorganize the Muslim League. Almost single-handedly he built the League into the broad-based political party that in the 1940's unified India's Muslims behind the demand for the establishment of Pakistan. In 1946 the Muslim League won 90 percent of the Muslim legislative seats across India, and Muhammad Ali Jinnah was the undisputed leader of India's many Muslims. The British had no choice but to take Jinnah's views into account as they made plans for India's independence.

Muhammad Ali Jinnah and the script of Pakistan's national language, Urdu, on the front of a five-rupee note worth about 21 cents.

At first most Muslims thought the idea of a separate nation was ridiculous, but during the late 1930's, millions of Muslims across India changed their minds. The change began with the elections of 1937, which the British held when they granted more self-government to India's provincial legislatures.

The Muslim League was still very weak, for Jinnah had not had enough time since his return to India to raise money or increase membership. In many areas the League could not even put up a candidate, and across India it won only 23 percent of the seats allotted to Muslims.

The Congress Party, by contrast, won large majorities and formed governments in seven of India's eleven provinces. Jinnah had hoped that the Congress Party would appoint several members of the Muslim League to cabinet posts. But the leaders of Congress declined to share power, and when they appointed Muslims to office, they always chose

Important Dates During British Rule

Late 19th century	The British rule the whole of India and bring railroads, telegraph lines, post offices, and new irrigation to the subcontinent; British rule also turns India into a dependent colony whose economic and political future is determined thousands of miles away.
1906	Seventy men form the All-India Muslim League
1910	The British hold separate elections for Muslims
1916	Jinnah's Lucknow Pact creates a brief Hindu–Muslim unity
1920	Gandhi becomes the leading force in the Congress Party
1928	The Congress Party opposes separate elections for Muslims
1930	Muhammad Iqbal advocates a separate Muslim state
1933	Chaudhry Rahmat Ali coins the name "Pakistan"
1937–1939	Congress Party governments alienate the Muslims
1940	The Muslim League supports the British war effort, and passes the Pakistan Resolution
1940	Britain promises Muslims the right to prior approval of a constitution for an independent India
1946	In elections the Muslim League wins with 90 percent of the legislative seats reserved for Muslims

from among those Muslims who remained with the secular Congress Party.

An angry Jinnah charged that the Congress Party chose only "show-boy" Muslims who were subservient to Hindus, and he warned Muslims that this was what an independence dominated by Hindus would be like. To make matters worse, some of the Congress governments made schoolchildren sing the Congress Party anthem, *"Bande Mataram,"* a Hindu song that many Muslims considered idolatrous. Other Congress governments gave tax money to Hindu colleges, and one government even closed several Urdu-speaking schools.

It was a turning point. Muslims everywhere wondered what their status would be in an independent India dominated by Hindus, and they began to see Pakistan as a better alternative. Throughout India they rallied to the leadership of Muhammad Ali Jinnah, for by 1939 he too had come to favor the creation of Pakistan.

As the president of the Muslim League, Jinnah was the only Muslim leader in India with national rather than local stature. One newspaper gave him the title of Quaid-i-Azam, which in Urdu means "Great Leader." The distinction spread quickly, and to this day Pakistanis honor Jinnah with this title.

In Lahore in 1940, on March 23—a day celebrated ever since as Pakistan Day—60,000 men and women cheered as the Muslim League passed the Pakistan Resolution:

Resolved . . . that the areas in which Muslims are numerically in a majority as in the North-Western and Eastern zones of India should be grouped to constitute Independent States. . . .

Gandhi promptly denounced the resolution as "absurd" because it envisioned Pakistan as including the whole of the Punjab and Bengal, even though each of these two provinces was just 55 percent Muslim. He also strongly objected to the division of India. But Jinnah told the crowd in Lahore that Muslims were not just a minority, but a nation, fully entitled to their own state:

Hindus and Muslims belong to two different religious philosophies, social customs, literatures. They neither intermarry nor interdine together and indeed, they belong to two different civilizations. . . . They have different epics, different heroes, and different episodes. Very often the hero of one is the foe of the other. . . .

During the ages, India has always divided into Hindu India and Muslim India. The present artificial unity of India dates back only to the British conquest. . . .

Muslims are a nation according to any definition of a nation, and they must have their territory and their state.

World War II

When World War II broke out in 1939, the Congress Party refused to support Britain unless it first granted India independence. By contrast, the Muslim League not only supported the war against Germany and Japan, but even contributed soldiers. In return, a grateful Britain promised the Muslims in 1940 that it would never transfer power to an independent India unless its constitution was first approved by Muslims.

This pledge solidified Muslim support for the war, but it also made it impossible for Britain to promise that India could become independent after the war, for the Congress Party and the Muslim League had not agreed on a constitution for an independent India. To pressure the British into granting independence anyway, Gandhi began a new campaign of civil disobedience in May 1942, using the slogan "Quit India," a phrase that Hindus shouted at every British man, woman, and child for the rest of the war. In response, the British jailed Gandhi for two years.

Shortly after the British freed Gandhi, in May 1944, he visited Jinnah at Jinnah's home in Bombay. Gandhi proposed that after India

Muhammad Ali Jinnah and Gandhi in 1944.   Pakistan Directorate of Films and Publications

became independent from Britain, a federation could be formed under which the provinces with Muslim majorities could govern themselves on all domestic issues. But it was too late for promises from the Congress Party. Muslims wanted a separate nation altogether, and the cautious Jinnah wanted the partition to come *before* India's independence from Britain, not after.

When World War II ended in 1945, the British Viceroy, Lord Wavell, proposed that an executive council govern India until its independence. The council would include an equal number of Hindus and Muslims, with all but one of the Muslims appointed by the Muslim League. But Jinnah refused to allow what he called the "Hindu"

Congress Party to appoint even one Muslim to the council. He claimed that only his Muslim League represented India's Muslims, and he demanded new elections to prove it.

The leaders of the Congress Party strongly objected to Jinnah's claim that the Congress was just a Hindu party. They insisted on their right to represent Muslims as well as Hindus, and on their right to appoint a Muslim to the executive council. But they accepted Jinnah's challenge of new elections as the best way to break the deadlock between their parties, and Lord Wavell set election dates for December 1945 and February 1946.

The Triumph of the Muslim League

The candidates of the Muslim League campaigned on just one issue: Pakistan; and they won a stunning 90 percent of the legislative seats reserved for Muslims. Now even the Congress Party had to concede the truth of Jinnah's claim that only the Muslim League could speak for the Muslims of India.

The election results of 1946 were a triumph for Jinnah and for the Muslim League. Not since the death of the Mughal Emperor Aurangzeb had the Muslims of India been so united and well organized. And what they demanded was a nation of their own.

CHAPTER VII

The Birth of Pakistan (1946–1948)

A Last Try for Unity

Despite the victories of Muhammad Ali Jinnah's Muslim League in the elections of 1946, the British did not want to divide India in two. In May 1946, Britain proposed instead that India become a federation of three large provinces, each self-governing except in matters of defense and foreign policy. Muslims would be in the majority in northwest India and in Bengal, while Hindus would be dominant in the vast province containing the rest of India.

The Muslim League initially accepted the plan as a "step on the road to Pakistan," but once more the Congress Party, the majority party in India, insisted on the right to appoint some of its own Muslim members to positions in government. This was intolerable to Jinnah, and at his request the Muslim League withdrew its acceptance of the British plan in July. Once again Jinnah claimed that only the Muslim League had the right to represent the Muslims of India.

Jinnah could not compromise on this point. He felt if he approved of the appointment of even one Congress Party Muslim, then soon hundreds of Muslims would be seduced by tempting offers of jobs in a Congress government. Muslims would lose their unity, and with it all hope of securing Pakistan.

This knotty issue of who could appoint Muslims to office kept the Muslim League from cooperating with the Congress Party even on matters of short-term administration. By August 1946, the British had no choice but to ask the Congress Party to form a preindependence government without the Muslim League.

Religious Violence

As logical as the British request was, it came as a shock to Muslims. They felt Britain was breaking its wartime promise, the promise not to relinquish power in India until the Muslims had first approved of a constitution. Now Muslims were fearful, for as they saw it, they would soon be governed not by the British, who at least believed in one God, but by caste-conscious Hindus, who believed in many. In 1,200 years in India the Muslims had never before been under Hindu rule.

Jinnah responded to the new Congress government by declaring August 16, 1946, Direct Action Day. It was supposed to be a day of strikes and demonstrations demanding the formation of the Muslim state of Pakistan. But in Calcutta, the local Muslim government gave the police a three-day holiday, an action that recklessly and probably intentionally insured that demonstrations would lead to violence between Hindus and Muslims.

The carnage that summer weekend was horrendous. Using iron bars, broken bottles, and kerosene bombs, Hindu and Muslim mobs in Calcutta killed well over 5,000 people and frightened tens of thousands more into leaving the city. A few weeks later, in the eastern Bengal town of Noakhali, Muslim gangs burned hundreds of Hindu homes and raped Hindu women. In response, Hindus in nearby Bihar province crying "Blood for blood!" rampaged through villages and killed 4,500 Muslims. The homicidal madness subsided only when Mohandas Gandhi walked from village to village and threatened to fast unto death until the killing stopped.

At the urging of British officials, the Muslim League agreed, in October 1946, to join the Congress Party government temporarily, to cool down passions. But Jinnah warned that more violence was inevitable, and that only the creation of Pakistan would bring permanent peace.

Often the riots had beginnings that seem trivial to Westerners. Hindus grew angry when Muslims ate beef, for cows are sacred to a Hindu. Muslims were furious when Hindus played music near a mosque, for secular music during prayer is sacrilegious to a Muslim. In such instances, many people who had suffered a lifetime of poverty and frustration suddenly burst into violence. In Bengal, tension was especially high because in many villages the peasants were Muslim, but the landlords and moneylenders were Hindu.

The Decision for Partition

In March 1947, the British Prime Minister sent a new Viceroy to India, Lord Louis Mountbatten (who would soon be the great-uncle of Britain's Prince Charles), with instructions to arrange for the independence of India by June 1948. Mountbatten was a war hero of royal blood and great charm, but his mission was difficult. Almost as soon as

Important Dates During the Birth of Pakistan

August–October 1946   Violence following the Muslim League's Direct Action Day kills thousands

March 1947   Britain sends Lord Louis Mountbatten, a new Viceroy, to India, with instructions to arrange for India's independence

June 1947   Britain announces its plan to partition India and forms a commission to draw the boundaries

August 14, 1947   Independence Day; Muhammad Ali Jinnah becomes the Governor-General of Pakistan

1947–1948   Almost 1 million die from religious violence

8 million Muslims leave their homes for Pakistan

6 million Hindus and Sikhs leave their homes for India

War in Kashmir results in the permanent division of the province

January 30, 1948   Mohandas Gandhi assassinated by a Hindu fanatic

September 11, 1948   Muhammad Ali Jinnah dies; Liaquat Ali Khan becomes the new leader of Pakistan he arrived, riots in the Punjab left 3,500 dead. Open civil war between Hindus and Muslims was growing more likely, and no one expected the Indian soldiers in the British army to keep from taking sides much longer.

Quickly, Mountbatten moved the date of independence up a year, to August 1947, in the hope of ending the terrible violence sooner. He also met with Jinnah six times during the month of April to see if there were any way to keep India united. But, as the Viceroy later recalled, "Jinnah made it abundantly clear from the first moment that so long as he lived he would never accept a united India. He demanded partition. He insisted on Pakistan." Mountbatten thought partition would be "the worst service I could do to India," but he reluctantly concluded that it was preferable to continued violence and probable civil war.

By the spring of 1947, even the leaders of the Congress Party favored partition. They had spent decades fighting for India's independence, and now that it was only a few months away, they could wait no longer. They knew they could never work in harmony with the Muslim League, and most members of Congress were now willing to lead a smaller India as long as it was free of interference from the hated League. In the words of Jawaharlal Nehru, who became India's first Prime Minister, "By cutting off the head we will get rid of the headache."

On June 3, 1947, the British government formally announced its plan to partition India into two nations. "Pakistan Zindabad!" ("Long Live Pakistan!"), Jinnah told Muslims over the radio that night. Their dream of a separate nation was about to come true.

Gandhi opposed the partition of "Mother India" to the end. He even suggested choosing Jinnah as Prime Minister as a way to keep India united. But the leaders of Congress ignored him, and approved the British partition plan by a 5-to-1 margin.

The Drawing of the Boundaries

The immediate question was where to draw the borders of Pakistan. Most of India's Muslims lived on the dusty plains of the Punjab or in the rain-drenched deltas of Bengal. But if the Punjab and Bengal became part of Pakistan, then the tens of millions of Hindus who also lived there would be trapped in a Muslim nation against their will. There was only one solution: the partition of India also had to include partitions of the Punjab and Bengal. Muslims hated the idea of dividing up their homelands, but they reluctantly agreed with Jinnah that a "moth-eaten Pakistan" was better than no Pakistan at all.

The division of the provinces had tragic consequences. Slicing Bengal and the Punjab in two meant that borders tore through power lines, railroads, and irrigation canals. In the Punjab, the new boundary split the homeland of the turban-wearing Sikhs in half, causing hundreds of thousands of Sikhs in Pakistan to move east to India to rejoin their brethren. Worst of all, partition meant that the jute farmers in eastern Bengal were cut off from the mills and docks of Calcutta. These already impoverished farmers would now have to pay customs duties just to get their crops to market. Despite all these difficulties, legislatures in both the Punjab and Bengal approved partition.

The British formed a commission of nine men and gave them just ten weeks to draw the borders that would split the fields of the Punjab and Bengal forever. The boundaries were not announced until the day after independence, and all the political parties agreed in advance to abide by them. The commission included four judges appointed by the Muslim League, four judges appointed by the Congress Party, and an English lawyer, Sir Cyril Radcliffe, who cast the tie-breaking vote on many occasions. The British also called a tribal meeting in Baluchistan, a legislative assembly in Sind, and a referendum in the North-

West Frontier Province to see what the people in each of these areas wanted to do. By large majorities, all three Muslim provinces voted to join Pakistan.

In Calcutta, merchants agreed to finance the construction of modern shipping facilities in the town of Chittagong, the small, sleepy city that was going to be East Pakistan's only seaport. And in Delhi, officials of the Congress Party and the Muslim League negotiated the division of weapons, military equipment, railroad cars, bank deposits, trucks, typewriters, and even paper. The division of goods was supposed to be in proportion to the population: 82.5 percent for India, 17.5 percent for Pakistan. Indeed, Gandhi fasted until everyone in the Congress Party cabinet pledged to send Pakistan its rightful share of India's wealth. Even so, East Pakistan received far less than its fair share of money, vehicles, and machines, and none of the machinery involved in weapons production ever left India.

Independence

After a century of British rule, independence came at last on August 14, 1947. In Karachi, which would be the capital of Pakistan until 1959, the newly arrived government was still in tents and lacked even a printing press. Nevertheless, the city cheered wildly as Muhammad Ali Jinnah became the first Governor-General of Pakistan, and the first Asian Governor-General in the British Commonwealth.

At the time of independence, the 900 miles that separated East and West Pakistan seemed much less important than the Muslim religion that united them. With 70 million citizens, Pakistan became the world's most populous Muslim country (Indonesia now holds that rank), and the fifth most populous nation in the world.

Migration and Death

The celebrations ended when the boundaries were announced three days later. In the eastern Punjab, armed Sikhs and Hindus killed thousands of Muslims with the specific aim of driving all the Muslims there west across the new border into Pakistan. They succeeded, but as the refugees streamed into the Shalimar Gardens in Lahore, Muslim gangs took revenge by slaughtering thousands of Sikhs and Hindus. This, of course, frightened nearly all the Sikhs and Hindus in the western Punjab into fleeing east to India. Everywhere law and order broke down completely, and even policemen joined in the killing.

Vultures filled the skies. Almost one million people were murdered in the religious violence of 1947 and 1948, more than the number of deaths suffered by all the armies of the British Commonwealth during World War II. Sometimes crazed gangs would hack to death an entire trainload of men, women, and children, leaving only a driverless train of corpses to roll silently on to the next station. In other incidents, peasant women who faced imminent gang rapes jumped to their deaths down deep wells rather than submit to such a dishonor.

Panic reigned as the violence fed on itself. The more Hindus were killed, the more Muslims feared retaliation, and vice versa. To avoid massacres, millions of families all over India emptied their homes, put their belongings in oxcarts, and trudged toward borders hundreds of miles away—only to arrive at crowded refugee camps full of disease. In all, six million Hindus and Sikhs fled to India, and eight million Muslims fled to Pakistan: the largest exodus of human beings in history. Gandhi tried to promote harmony by reading the Qur'an in public, and he continued to insist that Pakistan get a sixth of India's wealth. But his generosity angered militant Hindus, and one fanatic assassinated him on January 30, 1948. The murder of this gentle man shocked everyone, Muslim and Hindu alike, and it brought an end to the worst of the killing.

Throughout the turbulent years of 1947 and 1948, Pakistan's government struggled each day to prevent new violence, to save crops that Hindus and Sikhs had abandoned, to feed and find work for eight million refugees, to secure office space for new government departments, to win the trust of the Pakhtuns and Baluch, and to establish Urdu as the national language.

Muhammad Ali Jinnah also repeatedly assured Pakistan's non-Muslims that despite the waves of violence,

Pakistan is not going to be a theocratic state—to be ruled by priests with a divine mission. . . . Hindus, Christians and Parsis . . . will enjoy the same rights and privileges as any other citizens.

The Kashmir War

On Independence Day it was still uncertain whether the beautiful and autonomous mountainous kingdom of Kashmir would join India, join Pakistan, or remain independent. Over three fourths of Kashmir's people were Muslim; many looked kindly toward Pakistan. But the Maharaja of Kashmir, Hari Singh, as well as many of his subjects, favored continued independence rather than accession to Pakistan.

In western Kashmir, Muslim farmers who wanted to join Pakistan rebelled against local Hindu landlords and against the Maharaja's government early in October 1947. They were quickly supported by 5,000 Pakhtun tribesmen from the North-West Frontier Province, who arrived in trucks supplied by the Pakistani army. The tribesmen marched to within a few miles of the capital city of Srinagar, and had they taken the airport, they would have succeeded in bringing Kashmir into

Two Views of Kashmir

Since independence, India and Pakistan have fought in Kashmir twice, in 1948 and 1965. The two nations also have artillery skirmishes almost every year, and since 1990 more than 2,000 people have died in shooting between Kashmiri Muslims and the Indian army.

The heart of the dispute is the question of who should rule Kashmir. Indians claim Kashmir for four reasons. First, they feel Kashmir is legally part of India because its Maharaja formally joined the kingdom to India in 1947. Second, Indians claim Kashmir is vital to their nation's security, for without it, their low-lying capital city, New Delhi, would be vulnerable to an attack from the mountainous north. Third, Indians argue that Kashmir has been India's garden spot for centuries, and that its mountains and clear lakes belong to the entire subcontinent, and not just to one religious group.

Fourth, and perhaps most importantly, Indians feel that because Kashmir is the only province in India with a non-Hindu majority, its inclusion in India is vital if India is to continue as a secular nation, a concept especially important to many of India's 100 million Muslims.

Pakistanis respond with a single argument. The overwhelming majority of the people of Kashmir are Muslim, and they never chose to be citizens of India. Pakistanis believe that the Kashmiris deserve to vote on whether they want to be a part of India, a part of Pakistan, or even an independent nation. Since India has never allowed such a vote, Pakistanis regard the Indian presence in Kashmir as illegitimate and tyrannical.

Pakistan. But the Pakhtuns stopped to plunder the outskirts of Srinagar, alienating some Kashmiris in the process, and lost their opportunity forever.

The besieged Maharaja quickly signed an agreement making Kashmir part of India on October 26, 1947, and the Indian government flew thousands of troops into Srinagar the next day. More Pakhtuns from Pakistan also poured in, but it was too late. The Indian army drove the Pakhtuns back to about 40 miles (65 kilometers) west of Srinagar, where the war bogged down. India and Pakistan finally agreed to a United Nations cease-fire on August 13, 1948.

Since then, India has held the eastern two thirds of Kashmir, including the city of Srinagar and the beautiful mountain lakes nearby. Pakistan holds the drier and more sparsely populated western third of the province, most of which is what the Pakinstanis today refer to as the Northern Areas. In part of Pakistani Kashmir, however, Muslims have created the small state of Azad (Free) Kashmir.

Under the terms of the United Nations cease-fire, India was supposed to hold an election to see whether the people of Kashmir wanted to join India or Pakistan. But, fearful that the Muslims of Kashmir might vote to join Pakistan, India has never held the election. India insists that Pakistan first withdraw all of its soldiers from western Kashmir, but Pakistan refuses unless India simultaneously withdraws its soldiers from eastern Kashmir. Troops have remained along the cease-fire line for over forty years, and both nations continue to claim the whole of Kashmir.

The Kashmir dispute is a terrible tragedy for India and Pakistan. Muhammad Ali Jinnah had hoped that Pakistan's border with India would be peaceful and demilitarized, like the border between the United States and Canada. Instead, for four decades India and Pakistan have spent almost half of their annual budgets maintaining huge armies to defend their portions of Kashmir.

It is a catastrophe similar to the recent arms race between the United States and the Soviet Union; vast sums of money spent on the military might otherwise have gone toward schools, health care, roads, and sanitation. But the tragedy seems greater in India and Pakistan, where so many millions of people remain poor and illiterate.

The Death of Jinnah

On September 11, 1948, one month after India and Pakistan agreed to a cease-fire in Kashmir, Muhammad Ali Jinnah died of lung cancer at the age of seventy-one. His many years of chain-smoking and fourteen-hour workdays finally took their toll. In the last years of his life, Jinnah had relied increasingly on his longtime associate, Liaquat Ali Khan. Khan became the new leader of Pakistan. The one-year-old nation would have to go on without its founder.

CHAPTER VIII

The Loss of Democracy, The Loss of East Pakistan (1948–1971)

Starting With Nothing

Pakistan began its existence in 1947 as a geographical oddity. Not only were East and West Pakistan separated by 900 miles (1,450 kilometers), but the regions themselves had little in common but Islam. The heavily irrigated desert of West Pakistan and the rain-soaked Ganges-Brahmaputra Deltas of East Pakistan were, and are, as different in terrain as Egypt and Vietnam.

Another odd feature about Pakistan was that economic needs played no part in the drawing of its boundaries. In 1947 Pakistan had almost no industry, hardly any electric power plants, only seventeen cotton mills (India had 380), and not a single jute mill. The mills that turned jute into rope were all in India.

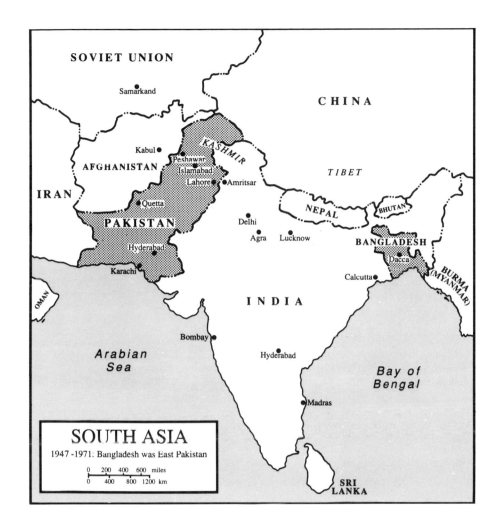

SOUTH ASIA
1947-1971: Bangladesh was East Pakistan

```
0    200   400   600  miles
0    400    800  1200  km
```

The new nation's biggest problem was that 10 percent of its people were refugees. Arriving from India, they needed food and shelter, and roughly half of them also needed land to farm. The government placed some refugees on land left behind by Hindus and Sikhs who had migrated to India, and put others on new, arid land that was irrigated for the first time.

Many refugees came from Indian cities. These Urdu-speaking Moha-

An East Pakistani woman sews bags at a jute mill in Dacca in 1963. United Nations

jirs streamed into Karachi, Lahore, and Hyderabad. Often it took years for them to find jobs and proper homes. However, the wealthier Hindus who left Pakistan had been bankers, entrepreneurs, and traders, and their absence created opportunities for the more enterprising Mohajirs. The strong international demand for Pakistan's jute and cotton encouraged many of these newcomers to start businesses quickly.

The Korean War of 1950–1953 was a boon to Pakistan. It drove jute and cotton prices up during a time when rainfall and harvests happened to be abundant. Foreign currency poured into Pakistan, and enterprising families began building factories to make rope, cotton cloth, and yarn, and other products such as vegetable oil, tires, paint, soap, and ink.

Political Chaos

For three years, Prime Minister Liaquat Ali Khan enjoyed wide support in both East and West Pakistan, for he had been Muhammad Ali Jinnah's right-hand man, and loyalty to Jinnah's memory was still strong. But in October 1951, a religious fanatic assassinated the Prime Minister, and this plunged Pakistan into seven years of political chaos.

Liaquat Ali Khan died before his government could draft a constitution for the new nation, which still operated according to British colonial law. Without his leadership, politicians could not agree on how legislative seats should be apportioned, or on whether Pakistan's central government should be strong, as West Pakistanis wanted, or weak, as East Pakistanis preferred. The National Assembly finally adopted a constitution in 1956, but it was in effect only briefly before it was suspended in 1958.

In the absence of a functioning constitution, there were no national elections in the 1950's. There were provincial elections, and there were contests for individual legislative seats. But there was never an election everywhere in Pakistan on the same day. Thus no political party could ever win a mandate from the people.

Six prime ministers tried to govern Pakistan between 1951 and 1958, but none held a legislative majority for long. Even the once-powerful Muslim League disintegrated into small factions dominated by conservative landlords.

Politicians traded favors freely, and corruption in the granting of building permits and import and export licenses became widespread. One politician's comment about an upcoming deal, as reported by a prominent lawyer of the time, was revealing. "I don't want to hear any ethical lectures," he said. "I only want to know if I can be prosecuted!"

The governments of the 1950's encouraged businessmen to build factories by offering tax incentives and interest-free loans, but they did little to help the farmer. They made few efforts to distribute seeds, fertilizer, or insecticides to individual farms. Worse still, the governments dampened individual incentive by paying farmers an artificially low price for their wheat. Not surprisingly, Pakistan's harvests in the middle and late 1950's did not keep up with its population growth. Food prices rose, the real value of wages declined, the economy stagnated, and strikes became common. Anxious and corrupt politicians postponed elections to avoid certain defeat. In the army, many junior officers openly advocated a military coup.

Ayub Khan

To bring order to a chaotic nation, and to head off revolt by younger officers, the commander in chief of the army, General Ayub Khan, staged a military coup on October 27, 1958. The general invoked martial law, army rule unchecked by civilian courts or legislatures, and maintained it until 1962. During these four years Ayub banned political parties and political activity. He also put corrupt politicians in jail, and he made himself President of Pakistan.

Ayub Khan's coup ended eleven years of unstable democracy and began a new era. Generals were to rule Pakistan for twenty-four of the next thirty years. In 1958, however, the overwhelming popular reaction to the coup was a sense of relief. People hoped that at last Pakistan would have a leader who made decisions in the national interest rather than for personal gain.

Most West Pakistanis today feel that as military dictators go, Ayub

Khan was a fairly good ruler. His elections were rigged, but his government was efficient, the economy grew, and he did not execute political prisoners. His Muslim Family Laws Ordinance of 1961 is still the strongest legal protection women have in male-dominated Pakistan. It generally restricts polygamy to cases in which a couple has been unable to have a son, and it prevents a husband from divorcing his wife without the permission of a local arbitration council.

Between 1959 and 1964, Ayub moved the capital of Pakistan from Karachi to a newly constructed city called Islamabad, which means "Home of Islam." Ayub thought Karachi was too vulnerable to naval attack, while Islamabad is inland and far from the Indian border.

Ayub Khan continued the longstanding government policy of encouraging industrial development, but he also helped farmers buy tractors and build tens of thousands of tube wells to irrigate new land. Most importantly, his government distributed the new, high-yield seeds of the agricultural Green Revolution: Mexican wheat and Philippine rice. Thanks to these seeds, wheat and rice production doubled in Pakistan during the late 1960's, as they did in many countries around the world.

A lot of money for agricultural improvements came from the United States. America and Pakistan were close allies during the 1950's and early 1960's, a time when the United States sought to "contain" the expansion of communism. In 1954, Pakistan became a member of SEATO, the Southeast Asia Treaty Organization, and in 1955 it joined CENTO, the Central Treaty Organization. Under these treaties the United States sent military aid to Pakistan and pledged to defend the country in the event of communist aggression.

One of Ayub Khan's youngest and most energetic cabinet members was Zulfikar Ali Bhutto, who became Foreign Minister in 1963 and later served as Prime Minister from 1971 to 1977. Shortly after Bhutto took office as Foreign Minister, he negotiated an agreement with China defining the border of Pakistan and China in the Karakoram mountains. This was the beginning of a close friendship between the two countries, for they both see India as a threat to their security.

The 1965 War With India

In December 1964, India announced that its acquisition of Kashmir was final. This was unacceptable to the Muslims of Azad (Free) Kashmir, and in August 1965, with the help of Pakistani intelligence agents, 7,000 men crossed the cease-fire line into Indian Kashmir in hopes of inciting a Muslim revolt. Indian soldiers then crossed the border into Pakistan, and by September there was war in Kashmir.

On September 6, 1965, India sent columns of tanks toward the cities of Lahore and Sialkot in the Punjab. The Indian and Pakistani armies fought fiercely in what was then the world's biggest tank battle since World War II, but after two weeks the United Nations arranged a cease-fire along the original border between the two nations.

The 1965 war did not change any boundaries, but it did have a number of repercussions. First, as soon as the war started, the United States temporarily stopped its military and economic aid to Pakistan. This shocked the Pakistanis, who had expected their ally to help them in their time of need. Thereafter, until the Soviet invasion of Afghanistan in 1979, Pakistan relied somewhat less on aid from the United States and turned instead to China and the Arab nations for support.

Second, the war crystalized the resentment that the 50 million people of East Pakistan felt toward the central government. Surrounded by India on three sides, East Pakistanis wanted friendship and free trade with India, not war. So they were appalled when their military and economic security were jeopardized by a war for a distant mountain province they cared nothing about. To the East Pakistanis, the 1965 war symbolized two decades of neglect by a national government dominated by West Pakistanis.

Dissatisfaction With Ayub's Government

The majority of Pakistan's people lived in East, not West Pakistan, and spoke Bengali, not Urdu. In the 1940's, many East Pakistanis had worked hard and had even risked their lives to support Muhammad Ali Jinnah's dream of a separate Muslim state, and after partition they had expected Pakistan to be a democracy. Instead, they were now subject to a military dictatorship in which 95 percent of the army officers and over two thirds of the civil servants were West Pakistanis. Few of these officials spoke Bengali, and many of them looked down on East Pakistanis for being short and dark-skinned. The budgetary decisions they made reflected their bias.

Over half of Pakistan's foreign currency was earned by the export of jute from East Pakistan, yet East Pakistanis received less than a third of the nation's imported goods. The majority of foreign aid and 90 percent of the defense budget were spent in West Pakistan, and partly as a result of this, West Pakistan's rate of economic growth was twice that of East Pakistan. West Pakistanis earned 50 percent more income per person than did East Pakistanis, and they were four times more likely to live in homes with electricity and to have access to hospital beds.

In essence, East Pakistan became a colony of West Pakistan. The sale of jute grown in the east helped pay for the industrial development undertaken in the west.

In February 1966, Sheikh Mujibur Rahman, the leader of the Awami (People's) League, East Pakistan's largest political party, demanded autonomy for East Pakistan. He called for East Pakistan to govern itself in all areas except defense and foreign policy, including even matters of

Important Dates During the First Years of Pakistan

1951	Assassination of Prime Minister Liaquat Ali Khan begins an era of political corruption and chaos
1958	General Ayub Khan becomes President in a military coup
1959–1964	Islamabad becomes the new capital of Pakistan
1965	Brief war with India
1969	Demonstrations and strikes force Ayub Khan to resign; General Yahya Khan succeeds as President and promises an election
1970	Cyclone kills 500,000 in East Pakistan; relief aid scarce
	The Awami League, demanding autonomy for East Pakistan, wins a majority of seats in the National Assembly
1971	Yahya Khan postpones the National Assembly and arrests Mujibur Rahman and other Awami League leaders
	The West Pakistani army's brutality causes 10 million East Pakistani refugees to flee to India
	India invades East Pakistan and captures West Pakistan's army
	East Pakistan becomes the new nation of Bangladesh

currency and taxation. Two years later the government arrested him on trumped-up charges of conspiring with Indian spies. The charges were soon dismissed, but the arrest helped make "Mujib" a hero to East Pakistanis.

By the late 1960's the East Pakistanis were not alone in their dislike of Ayub Khan's government. West Pakistanis were also tired of military rule. Intellectuals objected to the lack of democracy. Farmers resented the fact that their income was so much lower than that of city dwellers. And in the cities, factory workers and clerks, whose wages were stagnant, were angered by the vast sums of money accumulated by just a few families. In 1968, according to one prominent government economist, just two dozen families controlled two thirds of Pakistan's industrial capacity and over four fifths of its banking and insurance.

Pakistan's industrial output almost tripled in the 1960's, as cement factories, steel mills, fertilizer plants, and sugar refineries sprang up quickly. But too much of the wealth from this surge in development went to those who were already rich, including Ayub's sons. By 1968 most Pakistanis wanted greater equality of opportunity, even if it meant a reduction in economic growth.

In October 1968, students across West Pakistan poured into the streets and demanded democracy. They were urged on by the fiery speeches of Zulfikar Ali Bhutto, who broke with Ayub Khan and formed his own political party, the Pakistan People's Party.

By February 1969, factory workers joined in the protests. Industry came to a standstill as strikes spread all over Pakistan. In the rural areas of East Pakistan, law and order broke down completely. Angry mobs publicly executed landlords, policemen, tax collectors, and others they regarded as oppressors. Finally, on March 25, 1969, Ayub Khan resigned as president and appointed General Yahya Khan as his successor.

Yahya Khan Holds Elections

Yahya Khan declared martial law and promptly sent troops throughout the nation to restore order. Yahya then promised that he would hold a nationwide election late in 1970—Pakistan's first since independence—and that the seats in the National Assembly would be apportioned on a one-person, one-vote basis. For twenty years West Pakistan's share of the national legislature had been equal to that of East Pakistan. Now, for the first time, East Pakistan would have a majority of the seats.

Probably Yahya thought there were so many political parties compet-

A bridge in Dacca, East Pakistan, destroyed by West Pakistan's army in 1971. United Nations/ T. Hagen

ing for power that, as in the 1950's, no single group would be dominant. The army could then still play a major role as an arbiter of political disputes.

But fate intervened. On November 12, 1970, less than four weeks before the national election, a terrible cyclone (which Westerners would call a hurricane) roared through East Pakistan. It killed roughly 500,000 people and left millions homeless, yet emergency aid from the central government was small, late, and poorly administered.

The next month all the pent-up frustration from twenty-three years of West Pakistani domination came to the fore. On election day, December 7, 1970, East Pakistanis voted overwhelmingly for the Awami League, the party that demanded autonomy for East Pakistan. They gave the Awami League 167 of East Pakistan's 169 legislative seats, enough to form a majority in the 313-seat National Assembly and to make Mujibur Rahman the Prime Minister of Pakistan. (In West Pakistan, Zulfikar Ali Bhutto's Pakistan People's Party won 88 of West Pakistan's 144 seats.)

Constitutional Deadlock

The size of the Awami League's election victory was a shock to West Pakistanis. With his party in the majority in the National Assembly, Mujibur Rahman now sought to write a new constitution granting full autonomy to East Pakistan in every area except defense and foreign policy.

West Pakistani leaders were willing to decentralize many government functions, but they regarded Mujib's demand for complete autonomy as unacceptable. To Yahya Khan, Zulfikar Ali Bhutto, and others, the Awami League's program was equivalent to secession. A national government that could not print its own money or tax its own citizens was no government at all.

Bhutto declared that the Pakistan People's Party would boycott the National Assembly unless Mujibur Rahman scaled back his demand for autonomy. But Mujib saw no reason to compromise, for his party had just won the election on this specific issue.

Civil War

On March 1, 1971, at the urging of Bhutto and several generals, President Yahya Khan indefinitely postponed the convening of the National Assembly just two days before it was scheduled to meet. Mujib called a general strike to protest this denial of democracy, and within days the strike spread across the whole of East Pakistan. The East Pakistanis also stopped paying taxes.

Emergency talks in Dacca, the capital of East Pakistan, among Mujib, Yahya, and Bhutto accomplished nothing, and on March 25, 1971, Yahya and Bhutto returned to West Pakistan. At about the same time, 75,000 West Pakistani troops were flown into East Pakistan. Yahya ordered them to arrest Mujib, outlaw the Awami League, and crush the strikes and protests. In response, Mujib, shortly before his arrest for treason, proclaimed East Pakistan to be an independent nation: the People's Republic of Bangladesh (Bengal State).

The events of the spring and summer of 1971 are not a period that Pakistanis today like to read, write, or talk about. During that year, West Pakistani soldiers deliberately tried to terrorize the East Pakistani people into submission. They bombed Dacca, burned villages and crops, and raped tens of thousands of women.

Over the next eight months, 10 million frightened refugees crossed the border from East Pakistan into India. Indian Prime Minister Indira Gandhi (no relation to Mohandas Gandhi) warned Pakistan that her nation was too poor to absorb these refugees, and she ordered her army to prepare for war.

An East Pakistani family flees to India in June 1971. UPI/Bettmann

On December 4, 1971, when snow in the Himalayas made it impossible for the Chinese to intervene, India invaded East Pakistan. The East Pakistanis greeted the Indian soldiers with joy, and within two weeks the Indian army had captured all of West Pakistan's troops in the east. East Pakistan ceased to exist; the new nation of Bangladesh was born.

Yahya Khan resigned in disgrace on December 20, 1971, and three weeks later Mujibur Rahman was freed and allowed to return in triumph to Bangladesh. Pakistan's new Chief Martial Law Administrator was Zulfikar Ali Bhutto, the leading politician of West Pakistan. The shrewd and flamboyant Bhutto would lead a smaller Pakistan into a new era of civilian rule.

Pakistan Since 1971

When Zulfikar Ali Bhutto became the leader of Pakistan in December 1971, Indian troops had just split the nation into two countries. East Pakistan became Bangladesh, and West Pakistan was in shock. Bhutto, however, was uniquely qualified to help West Pakistan recover, for he had a genuine mandate from its people. In 1970 his political party had won a majority of the vote in West Pakistan, in the first election since 1946 that was both nationwide and free.

Zulfikar Ali Bhutto

The son of a landlord whose family owned over 45,000 acres in Sind, Bhutto studied at Berkeley and Oxford before serving in the cabinet of General Ayub Khan. The aristocratic Bhutto enjoyed French wine and

Zulfikar Ali Bhutto at a rally in 1969.   UPI/Bettmann

Cuban cigars, but he built his career by appealing to the people.
A great orator, he campaigned in 1970 on the simple promise of
"food, clothing, and shelter." His political party, the Pakistan People's
Party, organized chapters in the poorest slums and the most remote

villages. The voters responded and chose the charismatic Bhutto as their champion.

During his five and a half years in power, Bhutto made Pakistan's government more responsive to ordinary people by placing the civil service under the supervision of political appointees. He also put women in government jobs and expanded their opportunities to obtain secondary and university educations.

Probably Bhutto's greatest contribution was his role in drafting a democratic constitution when he ended martial law in 1973. The constitution set up a parliamentary system of government based upon direct popular elections, and it guaranteed freedom of speech and a judicial system with due process. Pakistanis continue to regard this constitution as their nation's proper governing document, although in 1985 it was modified, and many say distorted, by General Zia ul-Haq.

More than a decade after his death, Zulfikar Ali Bhutto is still loved by millions of Pakistanis because he spoke up for the concerns of the poor and was bold enough to make significant changes on their behalf. But Bhutto was hated by many people too, and three facets of Bhutto's character ultimately led to his downfall. First, he was tactless. He ridiculed his opponents mercilessly in public speeches, calling one politician a "potato" and adding a feminine ending to the last name of another. The poor people loved Bhutto's insults of the powerful, but the many politicians, generals, and Muslim clerics he mocked never forgave him, and they became his enemies for life.

Second, Bhutto's understandable resentment of Western global power blinded him to the advantages of private ownership. During his first three years in office, Bhutto created an "Islamic socialism" that cost Pakistan a decade of economic progress. Seeking to break the power of the two dozen families that had come to control so much of Pakistan's industrial wealth during the 1950's and 1960's, Bhutto nationalized banks, insurance companies, steel mills, utilities, chemical complexes, tractor factories, cement plants, flour mills, cotton mills, and many other businesses.

This new government control of industry was harmful in several ways. Wealthy Pakistanis began to invest their money abroad instead of at home. Even small businessmen grew frightened, wondering whether their firms were going to be nationalized next. Cautious civil servants were unused to making quick business decisions. Many newly nationalized industries came to a standstill, and total industrial production declined. Foreign investments also dwindled, and even today, a lingering fear of nationalization restrains some financiers from investing in Pakistan.

The nationalizations were symptomatic of Bhutto's third trait, his tendency to act like an autocratic Sindhi landlord instead of a democratically elected public servant. In the words of one businessman, Bhutto nationalized industry "not for socialism, but for power."

Bhutto created a personal secret police, the Federal Security Force, answerable only to him. Part of his reason for doing this was to give his civilian government a power base independent of the army. Bhutto quite rightly felt that the army had interfered enough in Pakistani politics. But Bhutto abused the Federal Security Force, and he ruthlessly used it to imprison and beat up hundreds of his opponents.

Although Bhutto made many powerful enemies, he remained popular with the poor. He began a small amount of land redistribution, gave greater freedom to trade unions, and also required employers to raise the minimum wage. Perhaps most importantly, he gave the poor self-confidence. Before Bhutto, for example, tenants in Sind had bowed and cringed before their landlords. But after Bhutto's rise to power, peasants began to stand up for their rights, and even to argue with their landlords face to face.

How Pakistan Built Nuclear Weapons

Pakistan today has all the components of an atomic bomb and can quickly make several bombs any time it chooses, according to Leonard Spector, the world's leading authority on nuclear proliferation. The bombs would be small enough (400 pounds, or 180 kilograms) to be carried inside an F-16 fighter bomber or a short-range M-11 missile, which means that Pakistan is capable of dropping a bomb on New Delhi. Pakistan has probably built the components for half a dozen atomic bombs since 1986.

India's army outnumbers Pakistan's by almost three to one. But what is more frightening to Pakistanis is that India has stockpiled dozens of atomic bombs since it first exploded one in May 1974. Pakistan has offered to sign the Nuclear Non-Proliferation Treaty and give up its nuclear weapons if India does the same, but India refuses, for it fears neighboring China, also a nuclear power.

Zulfikar Ali Bhutto once said, "If India builds the bomb, we will eat grass or leaves, even go hungry, but we will build one of our own." Of course, it was easier said than done. Less than 1 percent of natural uranium is radioactive, but to make an atom bomb explode, 93 percent of the uranium in a bomb must be radioactive. The problem is how to separate radioactive uranium from nonradioactive uranium.

Scientists use a method called "enrichment." Gaseous uranium is put into ultra–high-speed centrifuges, where nonradioactive uranium, which weighs slightly more than radioactive uranium, slowly moves to the outside of each centrifuge. The process must be repeated many times, and requires over a thousand centrifuges.

Pakistan built its uranium enrichment plant near a town called

Kahuta, outside Islamabad, the capital city. The man in charge of the enrichment program is Dr. Abdul Qadeer Khan, a metallurgist who was educated in Germany.

In the early 1970's, Dr. Qadeer worked at a uranium enrichment plant in the Netherlands, where he had access to a lot of classified information. In 1974 and 1975, Dr. Qadeer made several trips to Pakistan, duplicating on paper the design of the Dutch plant and providing sources of suppliers of parts needed for centrifuges.

In December 1975, Dr. Qadeer returned to Pakistan for good. He organized teams of buyers, who traveled all over Europe looking for the precision-made parts necessary to centrifuges. Sales were made to dummy corporations, and parts were first shipped to other nations such as Turkey. By the time European manufacturers caught on to Pakistan's ruse in 1978, it was too late. Pakistan already had the parts it needed to build an atomic bomb.

Pakistan's new uranium-enrichment facilities were far more modern than those of China, whose plants were modeled on Soviet designs from the 1950's. So China and Pakistan made a deal. Pakistan supplied China with the blueprints of its enrichment plant. In return, China gave Pakistan the design of an atomic bomb it had exploded in 1967, and also helped Pakistan test the nonnuclear components of its bombs.

By February 1984, the plant at Kahuta was enriching uranium. By autumn 1986, the uranium was weapons grade—over 93 percent radioactive. And in March 1987, in an interview with *Time* magazine, President Zia publicly admitted that "Pakistan has the capability of building the Bomb whenever it wishes."

The 1977 Election and Coup

When Bhutto ran for reelection in March 1977, his Pakistan People's Party had the clear support of a majority of the people. But many observers believe that some of Bhutto's supporters rigged the election slightly to make Bhutto's majorities seem larger. The official results were that the Pakistan People's Party won 68 percent of the popular vote and 77 percent of the seats in the national assembly.

Opposition parties charged fraud and held massive demonstrations. Led by conservative Muslim clerics who despised Bhutto's modern outlook, the protests grew increasingly violent and continued for four months.

Bhutto tried to meet the major objections of his opponents, agreeing to their demand for a new set of elections in October 1977. He also outlawed gambling, made it illegal for Muslims to drink alcohol (even though he drank himself), and changed the day government offices closed from Sunday to Friday, the Muslim sabbath.

By late June 1977, the number of demonstrations throughout the nation was dwindling, but it was too late. Army officers were tired of maintaining order on behalf of a civilian leader they feared and distrusted. On July 5, 1977, General Zia ul-Haq led a military coup and declared martial law. He promised to restore democracy to Pakistan in ninety days, but he never did.

Ironically, Bhutto had chosen Zia to be his army chief of staff over ten more senior generals in 1976. Bhutto had hoped to weaken the army's power by appointing a chief of staff who owed his position solely to him. Now, just one year later, Bhutto's nominee overthrew him.

General Zia disbanded Bhutto's Federal Security Force, promised new elections in October, and released the politicians whom Bhutto had jailed. They promptly traveled all over Pakistan, giving speeches. Bhutto also made speeches, and millions of people came to listen to him. A nervous Zia arrested Bhutto on September 3, 1977, on dubious charges that he had conspired to murder a political opponent.

Zia then canceled the October elections, saying that he needed to clean the government of its bad elements first. Zia's real reason for canceling the election was that Bhutto would have won it handily, and a victorious Bhutto would probably have arrested him.

Bhutto's Execution

For a year and a half General Zia kept Bhutto in a small, dark, unheated, and damp jail cell until a court made up of several of Bhutto's opponents convicted him of conspiracy to murder. On April 4, 1979, by Zia's order, Zulfikar Ali Bhutto was hanged. For all of Bhutto's faults, in the eyes of his many supporters, he had become a martyr for democracy.

Benazir Bhutto, the eldest child of the deceased prime minister, was a graduate of Harvard and Oxford and an unusually attractive young woman. General Zia feared that she might lead an opposition movement and had her imprisoned or confined to house arrest for four years, until in 1984 he allowed her to fly to London to get treatment for an ear infection.

The Afghan War Brings U.S. Aid

In 1979, the year of Bhutto's execution, food prices rose and the economy was stagnant. Opposition to General Zia, who now named himself President Zia, was so widespread that the government felt the need to execute 2,000 people and torture hundreds more. In addition, in May 1979, President Jimmy Carter cut off all U.S. military and economic aid to Pakistan because the Zia government refused to stop its drive toward building nuclear weapons. Without military aid from the United

States and without support from his own people, it was doubtful whether Zia could stay in power very long.

Everything changed on December 24, 1979, when the Soviet Union invaded Afghanistan. Eighty-five thousand soldiers of the Soviet army entered Afghanistan to prevent its one-year-old Communist government from falling. Despite their firepower, the Soviets could hold only the cities. In the countryside, at night, farmers and nomads banded together to fight back against the foreign, atheist invader. They called themselves the *mujahidin* (fighters of the holy war). (See *The Land and People of Afghanistan.*)

The war was brutal. The Soviets terrorized thousands of Afghan villages with helicopters, bombs, land mines, and machine-gun fire. Within a year and a half, 2 million Afghan refugees streamed into Pakistan, and another 1.5 million followed later. Four hundred thousand of them had lost an arm or a leg. They arrived on foot, in groups of fifty or a hundred: women, children, old men, wounded men, and healthy young men looking for guns. They settled in camps near Peshawar, the capital of the North-West Frontier Province.

The generosity of the Pakhtun people toward the Afghan refugees was remarkable. They welcomed the Afghans (many of whom were also Pakhtuns) as Muslim brothers, and they quickly built camps, where the Afghans received food, clothing, medicine, and shelter. Some Pakhtuns divided their homes in two and asked Afghan families to move in. "Hospitality is the way of the Pakhtuns," they said proudly.

In 1979, the United States had viewed President Zia as a dictator and an executioner. By 1980 America had new priorities. Pakistan was the "frontline" state against Soviet expansion in Afghanistan. Zia clearly had many flaws, but he was a fighter against communism and a helper of refugees.

The Reagan administration was generous. During the 1980's, the

United States sent $7 billion in aid to Pakistan. This included 49 F-16 fighter-bombers and 100 M-48 tanks, most of which were placed along the Indian border, not the border with Afghanistan.

Two billion dollars of the U.S. aid to the *mujahidin* was indirect. Food, money, and weapons first went to Pakistan's army, whose officers often took a cut, and only then to Afghan rebels.

As a result of this direct and indirect aid, the Pakistani army became even more prosperous and powerful than it had been before. Soldiers and officers had always eaten better food, lived in bigger houses, and earned more money than ordinary Pakistanis did. But recently the army has dominated more aspects of Pakistani life than it did in the past.

Army mills refine sugar and make cornflakes. Army ranches raise cows and sheep. Army trucks transport wheat. Army schools train doctors, engineers, and high school students. And army recruits build homes, spray crops, and sandbag riverbanks.

The most obvious example of army dominance was martial law, which lasted from 1977 to 1985. President Zia was Chief Martial Law Administrator. For eight years Pakistanis were subject to the jurisdiction of military courts. A defendant had no right to a lawyer, no right to a public trial, and no right to an appeal. In addition, the Zia government strictly censored the press until 1982, and enforced moderate press censorship from 1982 to 1988.

Islamization

During the years of martial law, President Zia began his program of Islamization. Zia was the son of a Muslim prayer leader in the British colonial army and was a genuinely religious man. He observed the rise of fundamentalism in Iran in 1978 and sought a program at home that

Before 10,000 spectators in Rawalpindi in October 1979, a young man endures fifteen lashes with a palm-wood cane as partial punishment for his involvement in a call-girl enterprise. UPI/Bettmann

would satisfy strict Muslims without driving away foreign investment.

In February 1979, Zia issued new laws that punished rape, adultery, and "carnal knowledge of a virgin" by stoning, first-time theft by the cutting off of the right hand, and drinking alcohol by eighty lashes. Despite these laws, which are still in force, no one has ever been stoned to death. Sentences of stoning have always been reduced upon appeal. Nor has anyone ever had his hand cut off. Pakistan's anti-theft law states that a doctor must amputate the hand surgically, and no doctor in Pakistan has ever agreed to do this.

Whippings, however, were not only performed in public during Zia's rule but were often televised, presumably to make potential criminals (and dissidents) think twice before breaking the law. The ends of the whips, however, were softened with padding.

President Zia set up Islamic Shariat courts to review military and civil verdicts and make sure that they were issued in accordance with Islamic law. He also revived the early Muslim rule of financial evidence, which gives a woman's testimony in monetary matters only half the weight of a man's, and applied this rule broadly, to every kind of case. There were also several thousand horror stories of pregnant women who accused men of rape but, failing to prove their charge of rape under Islamic law, were themselves convicted of adultery and sent to jail.

Discontent With Zia

The economy of Pakistan did well under the Zia government, often growing by as much as 7 percent per year. There were three reasons for this. First, Zia denationalized some of the industries that the Bhutto government had taken over, and they began to work more efficiently under private ownership. Second, there was an influx of American aid. And third and most important: luck. Almost all the wheat and cotton harvests during Zia's rule were good.

Nevertheless, many people chafed under Zia's strict, puritanical rule. In Sind province especially, people resented being dominated by an army that was predominantly Punjabi. In the summer of 1983, anti-Zia riots in Sind claimed the lives of 600 people and resulted in 7,000 arrests. Zia did, however, promise elections to choose a national assembly within eighteen months. But when the time came for elections in February 1985, Zia would not allow political parties to participate. He

Important Dates in
Pakistan's Recent History

1971	Bangladesh secedes; Zulfikar Ali Bhutto becomes the leader of Pakistan
1973	Ratification of the constitution that still governs Pakistan today
1977	General Zia ul-Haq overthrows Bhutto in a military coup
1977–1985	Martial law, Islamization laws
1979	Zia hangs Bhutto on a dubious charge of conspiracy to murder
	Soviet Union invades Afghanistan
1981	United States begins massive military and economic aid to Pakistan
1986–1987	Pakistan acquires the capability to build nuclear weapons
1988	Zia ul-Haq dies in a plane crash; sabotage suspected
1988	Benazir Bhutto elected Prime Minister
1990	President Ishaq Khan dismisses Bhutto's government; Mian Nawaz Sharif elected Prime Minister

also limited the powers of the national legislature. As in 1977, Zia had promised the people democracy, but he had not delivered.

Under pressure from President Zia, the National Assembly passed the eighth amendment to the constitution in September 1985. This amendment specifically exempted Zia and his regime from any future prosecution for acts in violation of the 1973 constitution. It also gave the president of the republic the right to dismiss the National Assembly at any time, for any reason. The amendment is still in force today. Despite its injustice, it may be one reason Pakistan's army allowed democracy to resume after Zia's death.

The Return of Benazir Bhutto

On December 31, 1985, President Zia lifted martial law after eight long years. Three months later, Benazir Bhutto, who had been living in London, returned to Pakistan. To everyone's astonishment, 3 million people greeted her at Lahore airport, showering her with rose petals and shouting *"Jeevay Bhutto"* ("Long live Bhutto").

The people were clearly tired of military rule, but it would take more than demonstrations to overthrow Zia. For the next two and a half years Benazir Bhutto worked to build up the membership of her father's political party, the Pakistan People's Party (PPP), and to strengthen its organization.

She also married Asif Zardari, a polo-playing businessman from a Baluch family that, like the Bhuttos, owns a lot of land in Sind. The marriage was arranged by their families, as is customary in Pakistan; the couple had known each other only seven days before agreeing to be engaged.

In May 1988, the Bhutto family announced that Benazir Bhutto was pregnant. Just four days after this news, on May 29, 1988, Zia dissolved the National Assembly. The elections were supposed to be held within ninety days of the dissolution, but Zia postponed them until November 16, 1988. Probably Zia chose this date hoping that Bhutto, who would be more than eight months pregnant by then, would be unable to campaign.

A Breakdown of Law and Order

Zia's excuse for dissolving the National Assembly was that there was a breakdown of law and order across the country. This was true, although it was hardly the fault of the assembly. The Afghan refugees brought thousands of AK-47 machine guns into Pakistan, along with tons of opium and heroin, giving rise to what is called the "Heroin and Kalashnikov Culture." (The Kalashnikov is the original Soviet-made AK-47.)

Much of the heroin that comes into the United States and Europe is refined by Pakhtuns in the Tribal Areas of the North-West Frontier Province, where the laws of Pakistan do not apply. According to several adventurous travelers, some of the drug dealers there are so rich, they live in houses with doorknobs made of gold and driveways made of marble. Other dealers have purchased enough votes to get themselves elected to seats in the National Assembly.

Smugglers ship some of their heroin to Karachi, where it has become so common that one out of every ten young men in the city is an addict. The spread of machine guns has also caused an alarming increase in robberies and kidnappings in Karachi, and to a lesser extent in other cities. Prosperous neighborhoods in Pakistani cities typically have an armed guard on each block, and a very rich family often has several personal bodyguards.

Karachi also suffers from ethnic violence between the sons of those who came from India during the partition—the Mohajirs—and native Sindhis. Sindhis resent the Mohajirs' economic successes, while Mohajirs resent job quotas that favor Sindhis. When fighting breaks out today, ethnic gangs fire machine guns at each other, so casualties are much higher than they were in the past.

In rural Sind even villages are unsafe. Thousands of bandits roam

Citizens of Rawalpindi protesting Indian rule in Kashmir honor the memory of Zia ul-Haq, who died eighteen months before this photograph was taken in February 1990.
Reuters/Bettmann

the roads at night, stopping buses and cars to rob the poor and kidnap the rich. Many bandits bribe local policemen and consequently go completely unchallenged.

The Death of Zia

In July 1988, President Zia announced that he would not allow political parties to compete in the November elections. Once again Zia was breaking his promise to restore democracy, for without the participation of opposition parties, the elections would be as meaningless as they had been in 1985.

But fate intervened. On August 17, 1988, Zia's presidential plane crashed shortly after takeoff, killing not only President Zia but ten of Pakistan's top generals and twenty-one others, including the U.S. Ambassador to Pakistan. The cause of the crash has never been determined, although investigations have concluded that sabotage was probable. Who might have done it, and why, is unknown.

In accordance with the constitution, the chairman of Pakistan's Senate, Ghulam Ishaq Khan, became the new President of Pakistan. The elderly and conservative Ishaq Khan had once served as Finance Minister under President Zia. Now he shared power with Mirza Aslam Beg, the new Army Chief of Staff and the only four-star general in Pakistan who had not been on the ill-fated plane. Together, the two men announced their intention to hold the November 1988 elections, as planned.

The Elections of 1988

On October 5, 1988, just two weeks after Benazir Bhutto prematurely gave birth to a son, Pakistan's Supreme Court ruled that political parties had the right to compete in the November elections. The new mother had only five weeks to campaign.

Millions of people, mostly poor and mostly pro-Bhutto, were unable to vote in the 1988 election because the interim government never gave them identity cards required for registration. Nevertheless, Bhutto's Pakistan People's Party won 93 of the 205 seats contested in the National Assembly. This was enough for the PPP to form a majority with the support of some small parties and independent members. On December 1, 1988, Benazir Bhutto became the first female Prime Minis-

A political cartoon making fun of a statement made by General Mirza Aslam Beg, the Chief of Staff of Pakistan's army, in August 1990. Far Eastern Economic Review

ter of Pakistan, and the first woman in modern times to lead a Muslim nation.

As a condition for allowing Benazir Bhutto to take power, the Army Chief of Staff, General Aslam Beg, apparently demanded two concessions. First, Bhutto agreed to keep Ghulam Ishaq Khan as President of Pakistan, even though he was not a member of her political party. As President, Ishaq Khan had the power to dismiss the National Assembly at any time, a power he exercised on August 6, 1990. Second, Bhutto appears to have promised General Beg that she would not cut the defense budget.

Benazir Bhutto thus became Pakistan's weakest leader since the 1950's. Despite her electoral success in 1988, she had to share power with two men: Army Chief of Staff Aslam Beg and President Ishaq Khan.

Benazir Bhutto's Year and a Half in Office

Benazir Bhutto's biggest accomplishment as prime minister was the restoration of democracy. Her government ended censorship, released political prisoners, and lifted regulations that had banned labor unions, student organizations, and political activity.

Bhutto's majority in the National Assembly was so slender, however, that her party could not enact any legislation. The rich continued to pay almost no taxes, and the size of the defense budget limited the amount that she could spend on education and health care. In addition, Zia's Islamization laws remained in force, so hundreds of women were still in prison for adultery.

Bhutto's biggest failure was the inability of her government to stop either the banditry in rural Sind or the ethnic violence between Sindhis and Mohajirs. Violence in Sind reached new heights in the first half of 1990, when riots and terror bombing killed over 500 people in Hyderabad and Karachi. This particularly angered the senior officers of the army, who worried that they might have to fight a war in Kashmir and a rebellion in Sind simultaneously. They asked Prime Minister Bhutto for emergency powers in Sind, but she refused to institute martial law in her home province.

In the top picture, Benazir Bhutto is a young student seated next to her father. Bottom, she is Prime Minister of Pakistan, and wearing a dupatta. Pakistan Directorate of Films and Publications

The Dismissal of Benazir Bhutto's Government

On August 6, 1990, President Ghulam Ishaq Khan dismissed Prime Minister Bhutto's government, dissolved the National Assembly, and scheduled new elections for October 24, 1990. Ishaq Khan did this just four days after Iraq invaded Kuwait, at a time when no one abroad was paying any attention to Pakistan.

Bhutto was not due to call an election until 1993, but the President claimed that the Bhutto government was incapable of restoring order in Sind. (Ironically, banditry and kidnapping in Sind have increased greatly since Bhutto's dismissal.) He also charged Bhutto, her husband, and some of her cabinet members with corruption in the awarding of government loans and contracts and the sale of public land.

Rather than appoint someone neutral to lead the temporary government and investigate charges of graft, President Ishaq Khan chose one of Benazir Bhutto's leading opponents to be Pakistan's interim prime minister: Ghulam Mustafa Jatoi.

The new government imprisoned Bhutto's husband, Asif Zardari, and set up seven courts to investigate the corruption in Bhutto's government. It did not, however, investigate any prior corruption during General Zia's rule or any recent graft by Bhutto's opponents. The evidence the government has presented to the courts against the Bhuttos and their associates so far is weak, and some of the charges have been dropped.

It is probable that several close friends of Bhutto's husband made money on a number of government transactions, but at this time it seems doubtful that Benazir Bhutto's government was any more corrupt than other governments in Pakistan's history, or that her husband really engaged in kidnapping and blackmail, as one indictment has charged. Yet under the rules of the court investigations, Benazir Bhutto and her allies are guilty until proven innocent, and any one court can disqualify Bhutto and her followers from participating in politics for seven years.

Strained Relations With the United States

When Iraq invaded Kuwait, Pakistan sent 11,000 soldiers to help defend Saudi Arabia. The nation's new leaders probably hoped to safeguard U.S. and Saudi aid, which was about $600 million in 1989. But the deployment of the troops was highly unpopular with the Pakistani public. After the Persian Gulf War began in January 1991, crowds all over Pakistan demonstrated in support of Muslim Iraq and against the United States and Israel.

Despite the presence of Pakistani soldiers in Saudi Arabia, the United States stopped giving aid to Pakistan on October 1, 1990. The U.S. Congress passed a law in 1985 that prohibits giving military or economic aid to any nation building nuclear weapons. In the late 1980's, when war in Afghanistan had made U.S. support of Pakistan a necessity, presidents Reagan and Bush had ignored Pakistan's nuclear weapons plans (as they have ignored Israel's) and continued U.S. aid. However, by 1990, President Bush could no longer credibly certify to Congress that Pakistan was not building nuclear weapons components. By law, therefore, U.S. aid to Pakistan stopped automatically.

The Election of 1990

In the autumn of 1990, Benazir Bhutto drew large and enthusiastic crowds wherever she campaigned, but she no longer had the advantage of being in power. The government-controlled television channel gave her campaign almost no news coverage. The new government also spent a lot of public money quickly building new roads and installing water mains, sewage pipes, and electricity and telephone lines in districts where voters were undecided.

On election day, the two main political parties competing were the Pakistan People's Party (PPP) and the Islamic Democratic Alliance (IDA), a coalition of nine political parties united against Benazir Bhutto. The largest of these parties is the Muslim League, an offshoot of the party of Muhammad Ali Jinnah.

The leader of the Muslim League is Mian Nawaz Sharif, the forty-two-year-old chief of Ittefaq Industries, one of the largest companies in Pakistan. Ittefaq owns four textile mills and a steel mill. The steel mill was nationalized in 1972 by Zulfikar Ali Bhutto, and then it was sold back to Ittefaq by General Zia in 1977. Not surprisingly, Nawaz Sharif has long since been a vigorous proponent of the reprivatization of many industries nationalized by the government. Nawaz Sharif served as a regional finance minister under Zia during the early 1980's, and as the Punjab's Chief Minister after 1985. In the 1988 election following Zia's death, the people of the Punjab voted for Nawaz Sharif to continue in office as the province's Chief Minister, making him by far the most powerful elected official opposed to Benazir Bhutto.

On October 24, 1990, the results of the national election were a surprise to everyone. The Islamic Democratic Alliance won by a huge margin, taking 105 out of the 207 seats contested, compared to just 45 seats for the Pakistan People's Party. Two weeks later, on November 6, 1990, the new National Assembly chose Mian Nawaz Sharif to be Prime Minister of Pakistan.

Benazir Bhutto charged that the government had engaged in massive election rigging, and her claim was supported by some, though not most, foreign observers. There was almost certainly ballot stuffing by the Islamic Democratic Alliance, and probably quite a few assembly seats were stolen. Even so, the vote padding did not necessarily alter the overall outcome of the election.

The 1990 vote, therefore, may be an anomaly. For the first time in Pakistan's history the conservative establishment of generals, businessmen, and religious leaders won a popular election. Why did so many Pakistanis vote against Benazir Bhutto? First, although Pakistanis expect corruption from government officials, they do not like it coming from the spouse of a Prime Minister. Bhutto lost some support because of her husband's wide-ranging business activities.

Second and more important, Benazir Bhutto was not effective enough in delivering the things that Pakistanis want most: roads, electricity, schools, and clean water. This is largely because she was a weak prime minister to begin with, lacking the support of army officers, civil servants, businessmen, and religious leaders. By contrast, Nawaz Sharif is supported by all these groups, so voters gambled that a strong government led by Sharif would be more likely to build the roads, utilities, and schools they needed than would a weak government led by Bhutto.

The Immediate Future

In spite of several decades of vote rigging, coups, executions, and ballot stuffing, Pakistan has slowly developed democratic institutions that even General Zia had to contend with. Now Pakistan may also be moving toward a somewhat stable two-party system with right- and left-wing coalitions perennially competing for power.

Much will depend on whether or not Benazir Bhutto is free to lead an opposition. Prime Minister Nawaz Sharif has said that the investigations into the corruption of the Bhutto government will continue, and in Sind province the Chief Minister has imprisoned over one thousand of

The Three Men Who Run Pakistan Today

As this book goes to press, these are the three most powerful men in Pakistan:

- Prime Minister Mian Nawaz Sharif, the head of Pakistan's government and the man who runs the nation's day-to-day affairs;
- President Ghulam Ishaq Khan, the experienced bureaucrat who supports Nawaz Sharif but nevertheless can dismiss the government and call new elections at any time;
- General Asif Nawaz Janjua, whom Prime Minister Nawaz Sharif appointed to be Army Chief of Staff when General Mirza Aslam Beg retired in August 1991. The commander of a large and loyal army, General Janjua could easily lead a military coup if he ever thought it was necessary.

Bhutto's supporters. But if government investigations focus only on Bhutto's administration, and if the police imprison and the courts disqualify only Bhutto's supporters, it will mean that it is not yet possible in Pakistan to lose power and be free from persecution. Harassment of a political party after it loses an election will only discourage future governments from holding elections at all.

Fighting in Afghanistan and Kashmir

Pakistan faces critical issues abroad as well as at home. The Soviet Union withdrew its army from Afghanistan in February 1989 and stopped shipping arms to the country after January 1, 1992. The Marxist government the Soviets supported, however, remained in power, longer than anyone expected.

Until 1992, Pakistan's army backed a faction of fundamentalist Muslim rebels led by Gulbuddin Hekmatyar, but he was unable to gain the support of the more moderate Afghan *mujahidin,* who also oppose the Marxist government. Hekmatyar has been especially disliked by the leaders of the once-Soviet and newly independent Central Asian republics, who are wary of Islamic fundamentalism. Because Pakistan greatly desires trade with these new nations, it has stopped sending weapons to Hekmatyar. Although fighting in Afghanistan continues, and 3.5 million refugees remain in Pakistan, a United Nations peace plan that includes elections is likely to be implemented soon.

War with India is also a possibility. For internal political reasons, the Indian government replaced elected officials in Kashmir with their own appointees. Harsh rule by these men provoked a violent uprising by Kashmiri Muslims, as well as several protests within India. Pakistan has given a limited amount of encouragement to the Kashmiris, which makes Indians even less inclined to support Kashmiri demands for self-government. Brutality by the Indian army has caused the deaths of over two thousand Kashmiris since January 1990, some by torture.

On July 5, 1991, Pakistan also removed an elected government in Kashmir—the first time it has ever interfered in Azad Kashmir so blatantly. The dispute centered on whether elections held in June 1991 were fair, but the crude manner in which Pakistan sent troops and arrested the leader of Azad Kashmir will cause some Kashmiris to wonder if independence might not be a better goal for their province than union with Pakistan.

Passions in Kashmir have been boiling for over forty years, but the situation is more dangerous today than before because India and Pakistan both have nuclear weapons. The leaders of these two nations will have to meet new standards of wisdom and restraint.

Daily Life

No matter who rules Pakistan, the daily life of the people changes little from year to year. A few fortunate Pakistanis live in spacious homes in well-kept suburbs, and travel abroad often. But most Pakistanis spend their lives in remote villages or crowded city streets, and work long hours growing food or laboring in factories, or keeping shops, or cooking, cleaning, and sewing at home.

Pakistanis commonly live in large families with five, six, or more children, usually sharing just two rooms. In rural areas children are useful as farmhands, but in urban areas children are an economic burden and make privacy impossible. Nevertheless, even in cities Pakistanis typically take great pleasure in large families. Whether they are rich or poor, Pakistanis enjoy the sound of children at play and the warmth of a crowded table at mealtime. A Western family with only two children does not strike most Pakistanis as being much fun.

A Village Home

Seventy percent of Pakistan's people live in villages. Most villages have between one hundred and three hundred families, each with around six to ten people.

A typical village home in Pakistan is a two-room dwelling made of a mixture of mud and straw, with wooden beams supporting the ceiling. It is cool inside. The roof and the walls have a mud-paste finish to prevent them from being washed away by rain. The floor is also made of mud, but women sweep the floor carefully, often coating it with a thin paste of water-buffalo dung and water. The paste acts like cement when it dries and does not have a smell.

A rural Pakistani home rarely has more than two small windows, for locks and railings are expensive, and only large landowners can afford glass windows. Consequently, the inside of a village house is dark, even during the day, and bare. Pakistanis have few possessions. Typically, a family owns a radio, a bicycle, a tape cassette player, and one cabinet with some plates, cups, and saucers inside. A wooden shelf usually runs along the top of a room, and on it is some brassware for cooking. Several rope beds crowd the room; they double as sofas during the day.

Three fifths of the villages in Pakistan have electricity. In such villages nearly every family has an electric light and either an electric fan or a ceiling fan. A few prosperous families also have a refrigerator and a black-and-white television set.

Even in villages without electricity some of the richest families own refrigerators and television sets—in anticipation of the day when electricity will come to the village. Until then, the families use their refrigerators as closets.

A village is often surrounded by a low mud wall. The fields are outside the wall, within easy walking distance of the village. Some fields are owned by individual families. Others are owned by landlords and rented to tenants in return for a percentage of the crop.

Inside the village wall, most homes are built side by side along a few narrow streets. Behind the homes are interior courtyards, often enclosed by mud walls like the wall around the village itself. The courtyard is where children play, and where a family's animals sleep at night. Typically, a family owns a pair of water buffaloes, a pair of oxen, half a dozen sheep and goats, and half a dozen chickens.

The courtyard is also where women cook over a small stone or clay

The inside of a home in a Baluch village outside of Karachi.   Mark Weston

fireplace built into the ground. Traditionally these fireplaces use animal dung and wood, but as trees and firewood have become scarce, butane- or kerosene-fueled burners have grown more common. The price of fuel, however, is high.

A Day in a Village

A day in a village begins with the appearance of the first light of dawn. Seconds later, a recording of the morning prayer call bellows out from a loudspeaker at the local mosque. Only about a fourth of the villagers actually begin their day by praying, but almost everyone gets up at this time.

Once out of bed, men wash themselves at a hand pump or by an irrigation channel, and women light a fire to begin cooking. The women do not wash themselves until after the men leave for the fields.

While some women cook, other women and children feed the animals. The oxen and water buffaloes each eat as much as 75 pounds (35 kilograms) of fresh fodder every day, including corn husks, wheat chaff, cotton stalks, and millet. The villagers cut the fodder each morning, so feeding the animals takes a long time.

Between six and seven o'clock the men yoke their oxen to a plow and start working in the fields while the day is still cool. The most common crops in Pakistan are wheat and cotton. While plowing, farmers often listen to the radio. They especially enjoy songs from movies. In both India and Pakistan, popular songs feature innocent, high-pitched female voices and low, melancholy male voices.

The richer farmers have tractors, but most farmers use ox-drawn plows when planting seeds. Similarly, during a harvest some farmers rent large combines to cut their crops, but most farmers harvest their crops by hand, with little more than a sickle. The threshing (separating of the seeds), however, is usually done by machine.

Water Buffaloes

Water buffaloes supplement the incomes of rural families throughout Pakistan, but especially in the Punjab, where there are over 12 million buffaloes. Even in some suburbs of Lahore, a Suzuki van may be in the garage, but a water buffalo sleeps in the front yard.

Pakistanis prefer water-buffalo milk to cow milk, and a female water buffalo commonly gives over two gallons (eight liters) of milk a day. A family can sell the milk for three rupees per liter (twelve cents a quart), which adds up to 24 rupees (about one dollar) a day, a full day's pay for an average farm laborer.

When a water buffalo becomes pregnant, which can happen annually, it is good news for a family. It means that their water buffalo will give milk for ten months until the calf is born, and for eight months thereafter, and also, of course, that the family will own another water buffalo.

A male water buffalo can be used for meat or to pull a plow, and might be worth a few thousand rupees ($100 to $200). But a young female water buffalo, if pregnant, is worth 25,000 rupees ($1,000). For a farm family this is about half of a year's gross income.

After the men have worked an hour or an hour and a half, the women usually walk out to the fields to bring them breakfast. Breakfast is most often a *chapati* or a *paratha*, served with butter and vegetables. A *chapati* is a flat, round piece of unleavened bread similar to a tortilla, but made from wheat rather than cornmeal. A *paratha* is softer and thicker. The men may drink *lassi*, a sweet, diluted yogurt made from water-buffalo milk, and sometimes they have tea.

Around noon the men stop to rest, often taking a nap. Then they may

Milking a water buffalo in a Punjabi village.   Mark Weston

work in the fields for another hour or two. Later in the afternoon the men gather under a large tree or at the village guest house to talk, to drink tea, and perhaps to have a piece of fruit. Most of the year, the afternoon is too hot for much strenuous work, although during harvesttime, men, women, and children ignore the heat and work from dawn to dusk to bring in a crop.

A woman's day is filled with domestic tasks. Besides cooking and washing dishes, the women of the family feed, milk, and care for their animals, wash clothes, and mend clothes if they need repair. If the women are enterprising, they may also make baskets or pottery for extra money. Many women work part-time in the fields, but their earnings are rarely more than twenty-five rupees (one dollar) a day.

Running water is rare in rural Pakistan, but many homes have hand-pumped wells. In these homes a woman washes her dishes and clothes outdoors, directly under the spout of her pump. However, millions of women in Pakistan do not even have this simple convenience. Instead, several times a day each woman must take a pot or a pitcher to a well in the center of the village, fill it up, and carry the heavy load on her head as she walks back home.

Though women often meet for tea at the home of a friend, the village well is their primary gathering place. Here women exchange news and gossip, and sometimes sing. Most wells draw water with an electric pump, but many older wells are powered by a blindfolded camel that continually walks in a circle.

Only a minority of children in rural areas go to school. Millions of young Pakistanis spend their days taking care of farm animals and working in the fields at half wages. When children do go to school, their education often ends after elementary school because a secondary school is too far away. And less than one child in a hundred in a village goes on to attend a university. Most young women get married at the early age of fifteen or sixteen. Their husbands, typically a few years older, have worked in the fields full-time since they were sixteen, and half-time since they were eleven.

Not every man in a village is a farmer. Many men work as carpenters, wheelwrights, blacksmiths, cobblers, tailors, potters, weavers, barbers, and rope-bed makers. Together they make the village a self-sufficient unit. Farmers commonly pay the craftsmen in food as well as in money. The sons of the craftsmen work as apprentices, usually following their fathers and uncles into the family vocation.

Many villages have kilns where brickmakers bake thousands of bricks a day. They work long hours in areas so hot that the fields are cool by comparison, but they are among the poorest people in Pakistan. Whole families make only twenty-five rupees (one dollar) a day, and slowly sink so deeply in debt to the local kiln owner that they can never leave the village. Their situation is akin to slavery. In the Punjab, one fourth of these brickmakers are Christian, descendents of low-caste Hindus who were converted by missionaries.

Evening

In a village, dinner is usually eaten at around six in the evening. Typically, two or three women cook for ten or more people, because often several brothers and their families live and eat together in a small compound. Like breakfast, dinner consists mainly of *chapatis* and vegetables, but the preparation is more elaborate. The women skillfully blend spices to create many delicious flavors, and except in poorer families, beef, lamb, or goat is served two or three times a week.

After dinner, while the women wash dishes, some of the men gather and talk. Other men listen to news on the radio; villagers are often knowledgeable about national and world events. The children feed the animals, for by this time the beasts are hungry again.

In villages without electricity, bedtime can be as early as nine o'clock. In villages with electricity, it can be as late as eleven. The only people with any real privacy at night are young married couples. A family will provide a young couple with a room of its own even if ten people have to sleep together in the next room.

Sometimes a young man must stay awake all night to receive irrigation water from a nearby river or canal. Water is a scarce commodity in many parts of Pakistan, and there are detailed district-wide agreements to make sure that each family gets its fair share of the precious liquid. Under these agreements, farmers divert water from canals twenty-four hours a day, and often a family's turn to irrigate its fields comes late at night.

Shortly before five or six in the morning, a shaft of light appears on the eastern horizon. The morning prayer call sounds, and a new day begins.

The *Shalwar Qameez*

Whether they are rich or poor, urban or rural, male or female, almost everyone in Pakistan wears a pair of leather sandals and a *shalwar qameez*. The *shalwar* is a pair of thin cotton trousers, baggy, but tapered at the ankles. The *qameez* is a long, cotton, pajamalike shirt that extends down below the knees. (The French and Spanish words for shirt, *chemise* and *camisa*, come from the same Arabic source as *qameez*, the Urdu word for "shirt.")

Among men, the *shalwar qameez* hides class distinctions, for rich and poor dress alike. A man's *shalwar qameez* is usually off-white or gray, although blue is also a popular color. The typical farmer or laborer has only two or three *shalwar qameez*, so his wife must do his laundry every other day.

Women wear the *shalwar qameez* in a wide variety of patterns and colors, and succeed in looking considerably more fashionable than men. In addition to wearing a *shalwar qameez*, a woman may cover her face with a veil, or she may just cover her hair with a scarflike shawl called a *dupatta*. In cities many women merely toss a long cotton cloth across their shoulders.

The *shalwar qameez* has long been popular in villages and among the urban poor, but educated people did not wear them regularly until both Zulfikar Ali Bhutto and General Zia ul-Haq made them popular in the 1970's. Bhutto wore the *shalwar qameez* to show that he was a

A father and his two sons wearing the shalwar qameez *in a mango orchard in a Pun-jabi village.* Mark Weston

man of the people, while Zia wore them to promote his program of Islamization. Zia ordered government employees to stop wearing Western shirts and trousers to work, and he discouraged women from wearing dresses that revealed their arms and legs. Women and government workers turned to the *shalwar qameez* instead, and by the beginning of the 1980's it had become the universal dress of Pakistan.

Pakistan's Largest Cities

Thirty percent of Pakistan's people live in urban areas, and they lead lives vastly different from those who live in villages. The majority of these people live in the seven cities of Pakistan that have one million or more people. These are:

Karachi—9 million; the seaport, financial center, industrial heart, and ethnic melting pot of Pakistan

Lahore—4.5 million; the city of Mughal monuments, established universities, large textile mills, and many newspapers

Peshawar—2 million; the commercial center of the North-West Frontier Province, a city of fruit canneries, furniture makers, and smugglers that today includes over 1 million Afghan refugees

Getting a shave in the town of Charsadda, in the North-West Frontier Province.
Diana Saint James

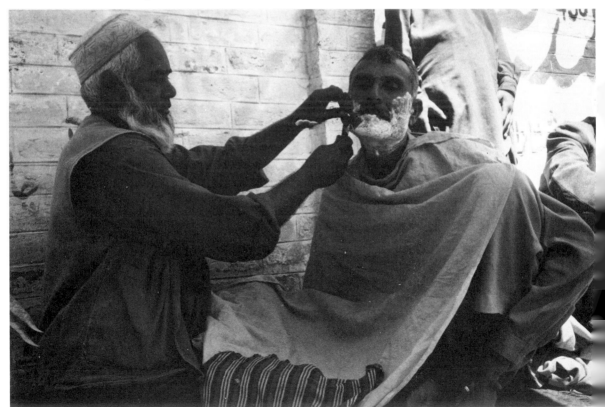

Faisalabad—1.5 million; the fast-growing industrial city of
central Punjab, with textile mills and fertilizer factories

Rawalpindi-Islamabad—1.5 million; twin cities, with older
Rawalpindi the headquarters of the army and the site of
textile mills, iron foundries, and a locomotive works, and
newly built Islamabad the capital of Pakistan and center
of the government

Hyderabad—1 million; the second-largest city in Sind, with
cotton mills, glass factories, and a bazaar over two miles
long

Multan—1 million; the dusty Punjabi city with many ancient
shrines of Muslim saints, a huge fertilizer factory, and
small cottage industries such as carpet weaving and
pottery making

City Streets

In few places in the world are streets as full of life as they are in
the cities of the South Asian subcontinent. Crowded bazaars, tightly
packed with open-air stalls beneath wooden houses centuries old, fill
one street after another, sprawling on for as long as a mile. In one alley
merchants sell brassware, in another spices, and in another flowers, or
radios, or jewelry. Along the sides of the streets vendors sell shish kebabs or spicy vegetable fritters called *samosas*. Others perform
acupuncture or sharpen scissors.

The streets themselves are jammed with every existing form of transportation: Japanese cars, pickup trucks, and motorcycles, brightly and
intricately painted trucks and commercial buses, crowded public

buses with dozens of young men riding on the roofs, bicycles (sometimes with a passenger riding sidesaddle), motorized three-wheeled
taxis, horse-drawn taxis called *tonga*s, oxen pulling wooden carts piled
high with heavy bricks, donkeys laden down with sacks of vegetables,
and porters carrying packages on top of their heads.

The sounds of the city include the high-pitched beeps of car horns,
the soft jingle of bicycle bells, the *putt-putt* of idling motorcycles and
taxis, the horse's clop, the donkey's bray, and the amplified voices of
the subcontinent's popular singers.

Away from the city's center, things are less crowded. The streets are
wider and are bordered by schools, government buildings, and bill-

A family of five rides a motorcycle together on a street in Karachi.   Mark Weston

Cars, taxis, bicycles, and horse-drawn carts weave through a busy street in Lahore.
United Nations/Wolff

boards advertising soft drinks and tires. Many cities have districts, directly run by the army, called cantonments. These are prosperous areas with suburban-style homes for army officers and businessmen, with good schools, parks, and well-paved roads. Most city dwellers, of course, live in much poorer surroundings.

A City Home

In a typical home in a Pakistani city, as in a village, a family of nine or ten people live in just two small rooms. Most families have a tiny cement bathroom and an outdoor courtyard or apartment terrace, but

Women fill their water jugs at a fountain in a poor neighborhood in Karachi.
United Nations

many poor families share both a bathroom and a courtyard with dozens of neighbors.

Houses are often made of cement blocks or bricks, with roofs of aluminum siding or cement, though some houses are made entirely of dried-mud bricks. Apartments are also made of cement blocks. Apartment houses are usually three or four stories high, and are painted a pastel color. The walls inside many homes are commonly painted a pastel blue or a light green, and cement floors are often covered with inexpensive plastic.

Married couples typically sleep on a bed, while children, depending on the prosperity of the family, sleep on sofas, rope beds, mats, or the floor. Generally several children sleep in the same room as their parents.

A family's possessions usually include some chairs, a table, a shelf with china and brassware piled on it, a ceiling fan or electric fan, a clock, a framed photograph of someone in the family, a tape player, a refrigerator, and a television set—frequently color, but more often black and white.

The kitchen is usually a tiny area with a cement floor. The burner and the sink are often in the floor, so when a woman cooks and washes dishes, she usually has to bend over or squat. In Karachi, only 40 percent of the homes have running water, and in some neighborhoods the water supply runs out by noon, so a woman must fill up several jugs each morning. In homes without running water there is often a hand pump in the kitchen. The water from a hand pump is good for washing,

A dentist's office in the town of Mingora, in the North-West Frontier Province. Mark Weston

but not drinking. For drinking water, a woman must take a huge metal jug to a faucet in the street several times a day, and carry the heavy jug back home.

A large majority of city homes are not connected to sewage systems, so waste often runs in ditches along the side of a street. In Karachi, the people of one neighborhood, Orangi, stopped waiting for an indifferent local government to help them, and built their own sewers. But this is an exception. Most urban areas lack proper sewage, and so diseases such as diarrhea, dysentery, malaria, and typhoid fever are common.

In thirty years Pakistani cities have tripled in size, and the government has not been able to build nearly enough housing and sanitation facilities to match this growth. Living conditions for most city dwellers today are crowded and unhealthy.

Children on a merry-go-round in downtown Karachi.   Mark Weston

Ironically, the chief cause of the overcrowding is also what makes it tolerable: children. The typical urban home has five or more children, and the typical side street has hundreds. With rare exceptions, the children have enough to eat, and they are full of laughter and play. So while many Pakistani slums have the squalor and lack of privacy of a prison, they also have the bubbly enthusiasm of a nursery school.

In addition, many more children go to school in the cities than in the villages. Even poor families often try to send all their children to school. A husband and wife, for instance, may make a humble living sweeping offices and homes, but they hope that if they live frugally and put their children through school, their family will be considerably better off in a decade or two. Their children give them hope for the future and pride in the upward mobility they have provided for them.

A Day in the City

City dwellers are more likely to sleep through the morning prayer call than villagers are, but most will nonetheless be out of bed by six o'clock. Showers in Pakistan are a luxury; bathing is more commonly done with a bucket of hot water and a cup. If a home does not have hot water, someone must heat the water first.

As in the villages, breakfast consists of a *chapati* (or a *paratha*) and vegetables, and, once a week, a fried egg as well. On many days the woman of the house does not have to cook breakfast, because leftovers in the refrigerator suffice as a morning meal.

Shopkeepers usually live within easy walking distance of their shops, which makes their twelve- to sixteen-hour workdays bearable. By contrast, factory workers, clerks and construction laborers work eight to ten hours a day, but they take a crowded public bus to get to work. A typical commute in the larger cities is forty-five minutes one way. For schoolchildren, however, a ride to school is usually less than ten minutes.

Buses are segregated by sex, with women in the front. Many women like the arrangement because it protects them from the occasional insult by a vulgar man. Bus drivers almost always have a tape deck at their side, loudly playing songs from popular movies.

At home, a majority of city women cook, clean, dust, wash, and do laundry without any modern appliances other than a small burner for cooking. Some women also work part-time as housekeepers, or sew or embroider at home to make extra money.

Men eat lunch at work, but children eat lunch at home when they return from school shortly after two o'clock. After lunch, children typically nap, do homework, and play.

As in the villages, a city woman commonly cooks dinner for about ten people. She serves meat more often than a village woman does, but usually she can afford to serve meat of high quality only once a week.

After dinner the women wash dishes and finish the laundry before joining the men to watch television. If a family is middle class they may watch an Indian or an American movie on a videocassette player, which is less expensive than a videocassette recorder. If a family is poor, they can watch only the one or, in some cities, two government-controlled television channels.

Young men may go to a movie theater, or just cruise around on a motorcycle. It is quite common in cities to see three men balanced on a single motorcycle. At night, the streets are almost entirely male. Women stay home in the evening, unless they are visiting neighbors close by. Dating is not a part of Pakistani life.

CHAPTER XI

Islam and Family

For fourteen centuries, Islam has given dignity and meaning to the lives of hundreds of millions of people from Morocco to Indonesia, educated and illiterate alike. Today one sixth of the world and 95 percent of the people of Pakistan are Muslim. Most Muslims in Pakistan take religion much more seriously than do most Americans or Europeans. There are proportionally far fewer agnostics or freethinkers in Pakistan than there are in the West. For most Pakistanis, religion is not so much a matter of individual belief as it is a matter of revealed truth and obvious duty.

Prayer

Perhaps a quarter of all Pakistanis pray five times a day. Many more pray at least once a day. The times of day when a crier, or an amplified tape recording of a crier, gives the *azan*, or prayer call, are just before dawn, just after noon, an hour before sunset, almost an hour after sunset, and about two and a half hours after sunset.

Before entering a mosque, men take their sandals off at the entrance. (Women do not usually go to mosques.) Then they wash their hands and feet at an outdoor basin before an *imam* leads them in prayer. A rural *imam* is usually a poorly educated man who, like his father and grandfather before him, teaches children to read the Qur'an, delivers sermons on Fridays, keeps up the grounds of the mosque, and presides at weddings and funerals. Villagers commonly call their *imam* a *mullah*, but in cities this is a somewhat disrespectful term.

In an urban mosque, the *imam* who leads prayers is more likely to be a *maulvi*, someone who is educated in the scripture and doctrines of Islam, or a *maulana*, a *maulvi* who has pursued studies at the highest level. Together, *imam*s, *maulvi*s, and *maulana*s are known as the *ulema*, or clergy, although there is no organized body of clerics in Islam, except among members of the Shia sect.

Prayers are in Arabic (learned by rote) and generally last about fifteen minutes. One of an *imam*'s most frequent sayings during prayer is *"Allahu Akbar!"* ("God is Great"). Worshippers face west by southwest, which from Pakistan is the direction of Mecca. Twice during each prayer, Muslims prostrate themselves, with hands, knees, and foreheads touching the ground. Many elderly men have prayed so often and so fervently that their foreheads have shiny indentations.

Holidays

Even Pakistanis who are not religious often fast during the month of Ramazan, or Ramadan, as the Arabs pronounce it. According to Muslims, Ramazan is the month when God first began his revelations to

Muhammad. During this month dutiful Muslims abstain from food and drink from dawn until sundown, and all public eating places are closed to Muslims during the day.

Each solar year Ramazan arrives about eleven days earlier than it did the year before, because the 354-day Islamic calendar is based on the moon rather than the sun. When Ramazan comes in the summer, daily fasting can be a long and exhausting ordeal.

A day during Ramazan is like no other time of year. Devout Muslims begin prayers at half past three in the morning (waking up the less devout) and then eat a big meal, called *sehri*, before dawn. Understandably, by two in the afternoon almost everyone is tired, and many people leave work early to take a nap. It is a fact of economic life in Muslim countries that productivity plummets during Ramazan. When sunset finally comes and the evening prayer call sounds, streets empty almost within seconds, and hungry people enjoy *iftar*, another large meal.

For those who are too poor to take a vacation, Ramazan is a major and often welcome break in their daily routine. The daily act of fasting also gives many people a sense of spiritual accomplishment and self-discipline.

When the new moon arrives and the four weeks of fasting are over, Muslims celebrate their second-most-important holiday, *Eid al-Fitr*. Like Christmas or Hannukah, it is a time of feasting, sweets, family reunions, and gifts of money.

The most important Muslim holiday is *Eid al-Azha* (the Feast of Sacrifice). This holiday celebrates Abraham's willingness to sacrifice his son Isaac in obedience to God's command. During this holiday, which also falls eleven days earlier each year, farmers and nomads throughout Pakistan make a great deal of money selling over 3 million goats to prosperous families. The families then sacrifice the goats to God and give one third of the meat to the poor.

Islam

"Islam" is the Arabic word for "submission," that is, submission to the will of God. The prophet Muhammad founded the religion of Islam early in the seventh century, in the city of Mecca, in what today is Saudi Arabia. Muhammad denounced his fellow Arabs for worshipping many different gods, and he preached instead that there is only one God, a God who will judge men and women according to their actions. (In Pakistan, whenever Muhammad's name is written, it is followed immediately by the phrase "peace be upon him," or its abbreviation, which in English is "PBUH.")

A Muslim is "one who submits" to Allah, and Allah is the Arabic name for the same God that Christians and Jews worship. Like Christians and Jews, Muslims revere the prophets of the Old Testament, but in addition they believe that Muhammad was the last and greatest of the prophets. Unlike Jews, Muslims believe in the virgin birth and miracles of Jesus, and also honor Mary and John the Baptist. Unlike Christians, Muslims do not believe that Jesus (or anyone else) is the son of God.

The sacred scripture of Islam is the Qur'an (also spelled Koran), which Muslims believe to be the word of God as spoken directly to Muhammad and recited by Muhammad to his followers. The book is divided into 114 *sura*s, or chapters.

The five chief duties of a Muslim are: 1) to make the profession of faith: "There is but one God, and Muhammad is his prophet"; 2) to pray toward Mecca five times a day and to pray at a mosque on Fridays; 3) to fast from sunrise to sunset during the month of Ramazan; 4) to give to the poor; and 5) to make at least one *hajj* (pilgrimage to Mecca) during one's lifetime, if one can afford it.

An elderly shopkeeper reading the Qur'an in the town of Gilgit, in the Northern Areas.
Christina Dameyer

Shia Muslims

Shia (Arabic for "partisan") Muslims, also called Shi'ites, account for 20 percent of the people of Pakistan, and over 70 percent of the people of the Northern Areas. Unlike the majority Sunni (orthodox) Muslims, Shi'ites believe that Muhammad's descendents should have been the hereditary leaders of Islam.

The most prominent holiday of the Shi'ites is the commemoration of the martyrdom of Hussain, the grandson of Muhammad, who was stabbed to death by rival Muslims in a struggle for the leadership of Islam. On the tenth day of Muharram, the first month of the Islamic calendar, Shi'ites march in long processions. Some carry a large replica of Hussain's mausoleum. Others beat their breasts and even whip themselves to reenact Hussain's suffering.

Sufism

Sufism is Islam's mystical tradition, emphasizing the love of God rather than the fear of God. It is a particularly strong influence on the South Asian subcontinent, because in the fourteenth and fifteenth centuries Sufi saints, called *pirs*, converted low-caste Hindus to Islam by the millions. Today, poor people who cannot afford a *hajj* to Mecca make pilgrimages to the tombs of *pirs* instead. Many Pakistanis believe that Sufi saints have the power to help them on Judgment Day, a belief that more orthodox Muslims consider a pagan superstition.

In rural areas in the Punjab and Sind, the descendents of *pirs* often own large tracts of land next to the shrines of their ancestors. The descendents are also called *pirs*—the saintly title is hereditary—and in general they are highly respected by the people of their districts.

Families

In a 1980 study of 116,000 employees of I.B.M. around the world, Geert Hofstede, a Dutch psychologist, concluded that Pakistan is one of the most family-oriented nations on earth. Most Pakistanis would readily and proudly agree. Pakistanis are more conscious of family

Last Names

This is a list of Karachi's most common last names, in order of frequency. Many of these names, mostly of Mohajirs, have their roots in cities in Persia, Arabia, and Uzbekistan:

Sayyid	Osmani	Zaidi	Shervani	Bukhari
Qureshi	Alvi	Kazmi	Shirazi	Barlas
Ansari	Hussaini	Rizvi	Isphani	Kirmani
Siddiqi	Jafri	Hashmi	Tirmizi	Yazdani
Farooqi	Naqvi	Abbassi		

A Sayyid (or Syed) is purportedly a direct descendent of Muhammad, although it is doubtful that this is true of every Sayyid. Many Mohajirs, for instance, added "Sayyid" to their names when they arrived in Pakistan and started new lives in the late 1940's.

In other parts of Pakistan many of the most common last names are titles, such as Khan, Shaikh, Mir, Sardar, Malik, and Chaudhry. As with Sayyid, not everyone who has a title for a last name is actually the descendent of a landowner or chief.

First Names

This is an alphabetical list of the first names of fifty-two men and women in one class at a business school in Lahore. Although these students come from prosperous families, their names are nevertheless typical of the nation as a whole. Many of them are named after some of the great men and women of Muslim history. Victorio, however, is Christian.

Men:

Aamir	Khalil	Omer
Abid	Khawer	Pervaiz
Ahmed	Mansoor	Reza
Akber	Maqsood	Saad
Ali	Mohd	Sadiq
Arif	Mohd	Sadruddin
Arshad	Mustafa	Shahzad
Azher	Nadeem	Sheheryar
Hafeez	Nasir	Shujaat
Hamanyun	Nasir	Timour
Imamat	Nile	Usman
Imran	Omer	Victorio
Inam	Omer	Yousaf
Jehanzeb		

Women:

Alliya	Saadia	Sara
Amina	Saadia	Shaheena
Humaira	Saira	Shazi
Naila	Saiqa	Tania

relationships than are many people in the West, and this is reflected in their language. In Punjabi, for example, some words have no counterparts in English, among them: *mamu* (mother's brother), *taya* (father's older brother), and *chacha* (father's younger brother).

The majority of Pakistanis live in large extended families that include parents, children, married sons and their families, and perhaps an aunt or a widowed sister. The father is the head of the family and is always obeyed, but sisters and younger brothers often defer to older brothers too. Unmarried children live with their families. It is almost unheard of in Pakistan for grown sons or daughters to live in the same city as their families and to keep separate apartments.

Often families also include the very old. Homes for the aged are nonexistent in Pakistan, and Pakistanis dislike the concept. One exaggerated image that many Pakistanis have of the West is that of ungrateful, materialistic children ruthlessly pushing their parents into nursing homes. This image reinforces the conviction many Pakistanis have that their families are closer and more loving than families in the West.

Marriage

In Pakistan, love and sex generally take place within the confines of marriage, and nearly all marriages are arranged by parents. Except among the very rich and very poor, premarital and extramarital sex are rare in Pakistan, for they are forbidden by the Qur'an.

In the countryside a woman is usually only fifteen or sixteen when her parents arrange her marriage, and a man eighteen or twenty. In cities a bride is more often twenty or twenty-one, and a groom about twenty-five.

Arranged marriages are seldom conducted between strangers. Half of all marriages in Pakistan are between cousins; the Western taboo against this does not exist in Pakistan. Many of the remaining marriages are between villagers or family friends who have known each other all their lives, or between a sister and a classmate of her brother at school.

There are some marriages in Pakistan, perhaps five percent of the total, where the bride and groom do not meet until the wedding. This is especially common in Baluchistan and the North-West Frontier Province. But even in these marriages the bride and groom more often than not see photographs of each other before their parents begin any arrangements.

In cities, by contrast, it is increasingly common for a young man and woman to spend several well-chaperoned days together to see if they like each other before anyone arranges a marriage. This is how Benazir Bhutto and her husband, Asif Zardari, first became acquainted.

"Love marriages" in which young people choose each other are growing in number, especially among university students. But they are still the exception, because romantic love is a dangerous thing in Pakistan. If a young couple starts a romance that does not end in marriage, the woman's reputation is ruined. There is no place in Pakistan for short-lived relationships.

At the other extreme, marriages forced by a father despite a daughter's protest are shrinking in number, but are still common. Unfortunately, if a Pakistani woman feels trapped in a marriage she never wanted, she not only is unable to return home—where the marriage was initially arranged—but is equally unable, in most cases, to move out and live on her own. Still, all in all, "An arranged marriage has its advantages," concludes Benazir Bhutto, whose mother arranged her marriage in 1987, just a year before she became Prime Minister of Pakistan. "You go into it without expecting much, and in a certain way this makes the marriage easier. In some cases the chemistry works."

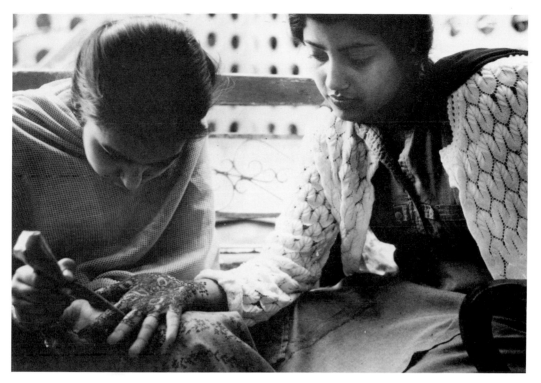

Brides have their hands decorated with henna the day before their wedding, but sometimes women have it done just to celebrate a holiday. U.N. Photo 154328/Viviane Holbrooke

Weddings

Weddings in Pakistan are expensive affairs, for hospitality is valued by all Pakistanis, not just Pakhtuns. At most weddings two hundred or more people have an elaborate dinner. Among the rich, guests often number more than a thousand. If a couple has four or five daughters, the expense of their weddings is likely to push the family permanently into debt. A bridal outfit alone, typically made of beautiful red and gold embroidery, may cost 10,000 to 20,000 rupees ($450 to $900), equal to several months' income in an average household.

For three days before a wedding, the sisters, cousins, and girl friends of a bride typically sing a mixture of traditional wedding and modern film songs outside the bride's home, and they also tease the groom with songs made up specifically for the occasion. The groom's relatives then reply with teasing songs of their own. Tea and sweets are served constantly, and everyone has a good time, especially the young, since a wedding is one of the few times that single men and women can mingle together.

On the last day before a wedding, in a ceremony called *mehndi*, the bride's hands and feet are decorated with henna, a reddish-brown dye that is applied in highly intricate patterns. The wedding ceremony itself is short and solemn, merely the recital of a few verses from the Qur'an. But soon afterward, the bride's sisters steal the groom's shoe and demand money as ransom. Since the groom cannot leave his own wedding with just one shoe, he offers a gift of money to his new sisters-in-law. Before he does, however, there is a lot of good-natured bargaining and banter. In cities, the ransom for a shoe can be well over 10,000 rupees ($400).

A bride brings her husband a dowry of clothes, linen, jewelry, cash, and household goods. In cities, the dowry is often also expected to include appliances such as a refrigerator, a videocassette player, or an air conditioner. Mothers start saving money for a dowry as soon as a daughter is born.

In Baluchistan and in the rural North-West Frontier Province, there is no dowry. Instead, the groom pays a "bride price" of cash to the bride's family, typically 30,000 to 100,000 rupees ($1,200 to $4,000). A father in these regions may marry his daughter to the highest bidder, even if he is also the oldest or least appealing suitor.

After a wedding, only the most prosperous couples go on honeymoons. Usually a bride moves right in with her husband's family, where she is expected to defer to her in-laws and do a large share of the housework. Some in-laws are not very kind to a new bride until she bears a son; only then do they fully accept her as part of the family. This is one reason some Pakistanis prefer marriages between cousins: A young woman's transition to married life is likely to be much easier when she moves in with relatives rather than strangers.

Divorce and Polygamy

Divorce is rare in Pakistan. It is slowly losing some of its stigma, but in general a divorced woman is still considered disgraced, so a woman usually seeks a divorce only if her husband is physically abusive. Men can seldom afford a divorce because of *mehr*, the promise of a bride-price that a groom makes to a bride's family before a wedding. Except in Baluchistan and the rural North-West Frontier Province, the groom makes just a token payment of a few hundred rupees to the bride's father at the time of the wedding. The rest is payable only if there is a divorce, and in practice this amounts to a fine that most men can't pay.

The Qur'an allows a man up to four wives if he can support them, but the Muslim Family Laws Ordinance enacted by Ayub Khan in 1961 prevents a man from marrying a second wife unless his first wife consents. This is rare unless she and her husband have been unable to have a son. Even then, most poor men cannot afford a second wife, and most rich men are too Westernized to want one. By and large, only a few landlords and *mullah*s in the countryside have more than one wife.

Pregnancy

Pakistan's population is growing by over 3 percent per year, one of the highest rates in the world, and less than 15 percent of the women in Pakistan use birth control. Many of the 85 percent of Pakistani women who are illiterate do not know that birth control is available. When women do want contraceptives, the dispensaries are often too far from their villages, and no agency issues contraceptives to single women.

In the absence of birth control, 50 percent of the women in Pakistan bear 8 or more children. (The average number of children a woman has, however, is lower, 6.7.) Many couples like having a lot of children because they are useful as farm laborers. And since very few Pakistanis have health insurance or social security, raising a large family is also the chief way for parents to make sure they will be supported in their old age. A family needs to have six or seven children to ensure that two sons will grow to adulthood, because 10 percent of Pakistani children die in infancy. Often they die of acute diarrhea caused by impure drinking water.

So much childbearing and child rearing can wear women down. Pakistan is one of the few nations where the life expectancy of women (fifty-one years) is lower than it is for men (fifty-two years).

Almost half of the pregnant and nursing women in Pakistan are anemic, and more than a quarter of Pakistani babies are born with a birth weight below 5.5 pounds (2.5 kilograms). This is true for three reasons. First, pregnant women usually need a lot of iron, but there is a deficiency of iron in the unvaried diet of many of the poor. Second, women who cook daily over smoky fires in small rooms often develop respiratory diseases. And finally, many rural women are exhausted by the hard physical work they do, which includes cooking, laundry, caring for children, collecting manure, gathering fodder, carrying water, milking, weeding, and, in the autumn, picking cotton.

Segregation

Unless they are relatives, or neighbors in a small village, Pakistani men and women spend little time together. Middle schools and high schools are segregated by sex, and young adults do not date. At night, the patrons of restaurants, movie theaters, and snack bars are nearly

Veiled women in Karachi.   United Nations/Philip Teuscher

all male. Even at parties adult men and women usually gather in separate groups. Educated women in Pakistan sometimes complain that many men do not know how to act with women, and see them only as sex objects. One woman in an office lamented, "I work with men, but I have no male friends. Men in Pakistan cannot conceptualize a platonic relationship with a woman."

There is little opportunity for men and women in Pakistan to learn to be friends. Not only is premarital sex unusual in Pakistan; so is premarital conversation. Unless they are studying or working abroad, Pakistanis rarely have a period in their youth when they live apart from their parents and develop friendships with the opposite sex independent of their families. To a Westerner it can seem as if young Pakistanis quickly leap from being children in the homes of their parents to being parents of children themselves.

Some women almost never leave home, not even to shop for food. They are kept in *purdah*, which in Urdu means "seclusion." This is common among urban, middle-class Pakistanis such as wholesalers and bazaar merchants because it is a sign of honor, piety, and status. Generally a poor woman in the country cannot live in *purdah*. She is needed by her husband or her father to carry well water or to work in the fields, and besides, in a small village there are no strangers to hide from. In the North-West Frontier Province, however, most women who work in the fields do maintain *purdah* when they are not working.

Although the Qur'an never mentions *purdah*, many women in *purdah* have nonetheless been brought up to believe that it is un-Islamic for women to have contact with men who are not relatives. They feel protected, and are grateful to be free from hard, physical work. But for others, *purdah* can be a prison. A woman who is beaten by her husband, for instance (or raped by a relative), sometimes cannot escape her home without incurring the wrath of other male relatives, who often see the maintenance of *purdah* as a matter of family honor.

Pakistani women cover themselves in public. The Qur'an forbids women to "display their adornment" to anyone outside their families. By custom and upbringing, most men and women regard the wearing of a veil as a basic requirement of modesty.

What counts as a veil varies widely. In the largest cities of the Punjab and Sind, a shawl across the shoulders is sufficient, although a scarflike *dupatta* over the head is somewhat more common. In small towns, however, and throughout Baluchistan and the North-West Frontier Province, women often wear a tent-like *burqa* that covers them completely.

Everywhere in Pakistan, women's dress is more conservative today than it was before the global rise of Muslim fundamentalism in the 1970's and General Zia's Islamization policies in the 1980's. During the 1940's, 1950's, and 1960's, for example, many women bicycled and played field hockey in short sleeves and short pants, a style of dress that would be unthinkable today.

The Future of Islam in Pakistan

Almost half a century after independence, Pakistan's citizens still debate the question of what kind of state Pakistan should be. Millions of Pakistanis, including many clerics, want Pakistan to be a theocratic state governed solely by the laws of the Qur'an. Many of them agree with Sayyid Abu al-Ala Mawdudi, the founder of Pakistan's strongest fundamentalist political party, who said that "for the entire human race, there is only one way of life which is right in the eyes of God and that is al-Islam."

The political power of the fundamentalist *ulema* increased greatly in the late 1970's and early 1980's when General Zia ul-Haq began a program of Islamization to win their favor and boost his weak public support. Today, thanks to Zia's policies, women dress more modestly, the drinking of alcohol is punishable by public whipping, and Shariat courts issue rulings on whether laws are in accordance with the Qur'an.

Counterbalancing the power of the *ulema* is a Western-educated elite of businessmen, journalists, army officers, and civil servants who want Pakistan to be a secular state governed by British legal principles. These men and women point out that Muhammad Ali Jinnah, the founder of Pakistan, was not a devout Muslim, and that he championed the rights of non-Muslim minorities and denounced *purdah*, among other customs, as "a crime against humanity." They see fundamentalist religious leaders as a threat to economic development because many of them want to apply Islamic laws to such things as modern banking, and to prevent women from entering the workforce.

Although many of the literate urban lower middle class revere the *ulema* as "the living conscience of the people," most Pakistanis do not want them to hold political power. Except for one fundamentalist political party, popular with Pakhtuns, religious parties have never done well in Pakistani elections.

A recent strike by bus and taxi drivers illustrates some of the conflicts arising between religious doctrine and daily life. For years, fundamentalists have sought to replace British common law with laws based on the Qur'an. One proposed law, the Qisas and Diyat Ordinance, includes a clause that makes anyone involved in an accident financially liable even if he or she was not negligent in any way. Although it is debatable how closely a law from seventh-century Arabia should apply to modern traffic, few politicians in Pakistan had the courage to oppose the new ordinance, for fear of appearing un-Islamic.

In disgust, Pakistan's bus and taxi drivers finally went on a brief strike in November 1990, to protest the possibility of their being liable for accidents in which they are not at fault. As a result of the strike, the section of the Qisas and Diyat Ordinance dealing with accidents did not become law, and, more important, a limit was set by ordinary citizens as to how far they will change their daily lives to suit one group's interpretation of the Qur'an.

A dormant but ultimately more serious religious controversy involves the rights of women. In sheer numbers, more women go to school and hold jobs than ever before. The growth in women's education stems partly from an enormous need in Muslim nations for female teachers and doctors, because schools and clinics are segregated by sex. But today, even unambitious women often complete their education because they know that educated men increasingly prefer educated wives.

The challenge for educated women who seek greater freedom and opportunity in Pakistan will be to separate patriarchy from Islam. This will be difficult, for Pakistanis will not change the many laws and customs that make men dominant in matters of family, employment, and property if they see the reforms as threatening Islam.

At present there is no Islamic feminist movement in Pakistan. Yet in the seventh century Muhammad himself fought for the right of women to get an education, to marry whom they chose, and to inherit property. Over the centuries, people have interpreted the Qur'an in ways that have narrowed the rights of women. But a new emphasis by women on some of the original verses of the Qur'an might be helpful to many Pakistanis who are trying to adjust to modern life without losing their identity as Muslims.

The majority of Pakistanis want to share in the material prosperity of the West, and they do not want narrow interpretations of the Qur'an to block economic progress. But they also want their children to be good Muslims, and they are afraid of the materialism and decadence that prosperity can bring. The role that Islam will play in Pakistan's future therefore depends on whether Pakistanis think Islam is secure in the face of the Western world's many influences.

If Pakistanis feel an alien culture is threatening their way of life, then they may give more power to the *ulema* in order to safeguard the basic virtues of their religion. But if they feel that modernization can enrich their lives without endangering their faith, then they may keep the fundamentalists in check and gradually foster some of the social changes that accompany economic growth. The kind of Islam and the pace of modernization that the people of Pakistan choose for themselves is likely to be influenced by events in the Middle East as well as at home, and also by whether Pakistanis feel the Muslim world is getting the respect from the West that they think it deserves.

The Economy

Although Pakistan is more prosperous than India and China, it is still one of the poorest nations in the world outside of Africa. Its per-capita income is just a little over $400 a year. If one subtracts public and corporate revenues from this figure, the household income for a typical Pakistani family of seven, which usually includes two adult workers, is only about 2,200 rupees ($90) a month.

Money buys more in Pakistan than it does in the West, as in all countries where wages are low. But the actual buying power of an ordinary family in Pakistan is less than half that of a family in Mexico.

Pakistan has so little industry that its gross national product (the yearly value of its goods and services, about $40 billion) is smaller than the annual sales of General Electric. Yet the nation succeeds in housing, clothing, and adequately feeding almost all of its 115 million people.

Economic Mini Facts

PAKISTAN'S TOP TEN EXPORTS   PAKISTAN'S TOP TEN IMPORTS

(By monetary value, 1988–1989)

PAKISTAN'S TOP TEN EXPORTS	PAKISTAN'S TOP TEN IMPORTS
1) Raw cotton	1) Machinery
2) Cotton yarn	2) Petroleum products and crude oil
3) Cotton fabrics	3) Chemicals
4) Cotton clothing	4) Vegetable oils
5) Rice	5) Motor vehicles
6) Leather	6) Unmilled wheat
7) Carpets	7) Iron and steel
8) Other textiles	8) Fertilizer
9) Cotton hosiery (stockings)	9) Tea
10) Cotton towels	10) Paper and cardboard

Source: Pakistan Federal Bureau of Statistics and Economic Advisor's Wing

Land Ownership

Over 50 percent of adult Pakistanis are farmers, a figure comparable to that of America in the 1890's. The average farmer and his family own just 13 acres (5.25 hectares). They grow two crops and earn about 50,000 rupees ($2,000) a year. By the time they pay for loans, seeds, pesticides, fuel, fertilizer, maintenance, repairs, and irrigation, however, there is little money left.

Farmers who own land are considerably better off than tenant farmers, who don't. One third of Pakistan's farmers are tenant farmers, including almost half of the farmers in Sind. Tenant farmers give half of what they grow to landlords, and therefore they have much less incentive than landowning farmers do to work hard or to spend money on improved seeds or fertilizer. Not surprisingly, crop yields per acre on tenant-cultivated farms are lower than those on owner-cultivated farms.

Most landlords protect their tenants from government abuse and lend them money in times of emergency. Few landlords help their tenants to get an education or break out of poverty.

The province of Sind is especially feudal. A tenant farmer in Sind is called a *hari*, and a Sindhi landlord regularly refers to his tenants as "my *hari*s." The landlords of Sind often have close relations with the local police. If tenants are difficult, the police may falsely accuse them of a crime; the landlord will then intervene on his tenants' behalf, with the understanding that they will cease to be troublesome in the future.

To promote equality and increase productivity, the government enacted land-reform laws in 1959 and 1972 so that no one could own more than a few hundred acres of land. Unfortunately, the laws had no teeth. Landlords deeded excess land to relatives, and nothing changed. Today almost two fifths of the farmland in Pakistan is still worked by tenant farmers.

Wheat

Wheat is Pakistan's most important crop. Farmers grow wheat not so much for the money it brings, but for food in the coming year. Keeping wheat in storage means that a family does not have to spend much money. Instead, once in a while a family brings some wheat to the local miller, and in exchange for a small percentage of the wheat, the miller grinds it into flour. Village artisans who take wheat or other kinds of food as payment for services include rope-bed makers, basket weavers, carpenters, potters, wheelwrights, shoemakers, tailors, and blacksmiths.

A Farmer's Tasks

Seed preparation
Plowing
Sowing
Collecting animal manure
Applying animal manure
Spreading chemical fertilizer
Maintaining storage sheds
Weeding

Harvesting
Binding or husking
Threshing (seed removal)
Drying (if necessary)
Transporting the crop
Selling the crop
Storing food for home use

In October or early November, farmers harness their cattle to plows and plant wheat on nearly half the cropland in Pakistan. They look after the wheat for six months until at last, in April or May, the wheat is tall, dense, golden, and ready for harvest.

Pakistan grows about 15 million tons of wheat a year, more than the output of Kansas and Nebraska combined. Yet this is barely enough to feed Pakistan's huge population. In most years the government has to import a small amount of wheat to keep its reserve stocks full.

Cotton

Cotton is the second-most-important crop in Pakistan, and the crop that earns the most money. The sales of raw cotton, and cotton yarn, fabric, garments, towels, stockings, and canvas, account for about 60 percent of the nation's exports. Pakistan is the world's fifth-largest producer of cotton, growing more cotton than all of the southern United States east of Texas.

Farmers usually plant cotton in May, just after the wheat harvest. Over the next several months the soil is irrigated five to eight times, until at last in October or November the cotton is ready for picking. Most cotton in Pakistan is painstakingly picked by hand, by women, not men.

Each year the entire Pakistani economy is affected by the size of the wheat and cotton crops. If rain is plentiful and harvests are abundant, everyone shares in prosperity. If rainfall is low and harvests are small, everyone's income declines. The government protects farmers by buying crops at prices that are often higher than international levels, but during a poor harvest this support is of limited value. Government purchases, however, help farmers to sell their crops quickly and avoid storage costs.

Sugar

Many farmers grow sugarcane, like wheat, mostly for their own use. They plant sugarcane in March, and irrigate the soil sixteen times before it is finally ready to be cut by hand in the autumn. Once the sugarcane is cut, Pakistan's farmers sell 40 percent of it to sugar mills. They keep the rest and crush it with a grindstone turned endlessly by an ox or a camel.

Farmers collect the juice from the crushed sugarcane and pour it into a giant pan four to five feet wide. They heat this pan over a roaring fire, fueled by the husks of the cane just crushed by the grindstone. Gradually, the hot, sweet juice solidifies into a yellow powder called *gur* that tastes like molasses. Even the poorest villagers have an adequate supply of *gur*.

Other Crops

On one tenth of the nation's cropland, Pakistani farmers grow rice from May to October. Paddies are particularly common along the irrigation canals of Sind province, and in the northeast corner of the Punjab, where rainfall is relatively abundant. Harvesting rice is hard work. Farmers bend low, with their feet ankle deep in water, and cut shoots of rice by hand with a sickle.

Other important crops in Pakistan are millet, a grain used as animal fodder that is coarser than wheat and thrives on dry land; corn, which serves both as food and as animal fodder; tobacco, common in the North-West Frontier Province; and lentils, the main ingredient in *dhal*, a spicy porridge that is one of Pakistan's most common foods.

Vegetables such as cauliflower, carrots, chilies, peas, and cucumbers perish quickly, so farmers grow them in quantity on the outskirts of towns and cities. From there they can quickly move the produce to nearby bazaars, while it is still fresh.

In the cooler highlands of Baluchistan and the North-West Frontier Province, farmers keep orchards of apricots, peaches, and pears. In the warmer Punjab, farmers grow citrus fruits and mangoes, and in Sind, a nearly tropical sun allows farmers to raise lush groves of date palms, bananas, and more mangoes.

Pakistani farmers grow five different kinds of mustard, so bright-yellow mustard fields are a beautiful and common sight. Other oilseeds grown in Pakistan are sesame, linseed, cotton seed, rapeseed, safflower, and sunflower.

Livestock

About 40 percent of Pakistan's families own livestock, and in Baluchistan the herding of sheep and goats is the most common means of livelihood. A typical rural family owns ten animals, not including chickens.

Water buffaloes provide families with milk, sheep furnish them with wool, and oxen pull plows. Only an eighth of Pakistan's farmers regularly plow with tractors rather than with cattle; another eighth of the nation's farmers use tractors occasionally. Pakistanis kill goats for meat year-round, but they slaughter them in especially large numbers during *Eid al-Azha*, the Muslim holiday. Cattle and sheep are also killed for meat, but meat is an expensive commodity. Almost half of Pakistan's families cannot afford to eat it more than once a week.

A large cotton-textile mill in Multan.   Pakistan Directorate of Films and Publications

Agriculture-Related Industries

Forty percent of Pakistan's industry is located in Karachi, but everywhere Pakistan's industry is primarily based on agriculture. The three largest industries are cotton-textile manufacturing, food processing, and fertilizer production. Together they account for more than half of Pakistan's industrial output.

In 1947, Pakistan had just 17 cotton-textile mills. Today it has over 150. Pakistan also has over 75 vegetable-oil factories (still not enough to meet domestic needs), 45 sugar mills, 9 large plants that turn natural gas into fertilizer, and dozens of flour mills, rice mills, wool-spinning mills, and cigarette factories. Many of these enterprises are government owned—nationalized in the 1970's by Zulfikar Ali Bhutto.

Cotton-textile manufacturing is by far Pakistan's largest industry. One fourth of the nation's industrial workers operate mechanical looms and spindles, and the yarn, fabric, stockings, clothes, and towels they produce make up two fifths of Pakistan's exports.

Other Large Industries

Pakistan has several steel mills, including one giant government-owned plant east of Karachi that was built with Soviet assistance in the 1960's. These mills enable Pakistan to produce almost, but not quite, all the steel it needs. Similarly, the 6 percent of Pakistan's industrial workers who work in chemical factories make the nation nearly self-sufficient in items such as paint, dye, varnish, insecticides, and soap. This is vital to the nation's economy, for Pakistan saves precious foreign currency by not having to import more steel and chemicals than it already does.

Other important industries in Pakistan include the making of surgical instruments, glass, sewing machines, and bicycles.

Motor Vehicles

Suzuki cars, vans, and pickup trucks are sometimes called Japan's gift to the developing world. They get excellent mileage and are easy to repair even when spare parts are not available. Suzuki builds its engines and two thirds of its parts in Japan, but it buys one third of its parts from over three hundred Pakistani suppliers. Then it assembles the vehicles at a large factory east of Karachi. Because the cars, vans, and pickup trucks are assembled in Pakistan, Suzuki's products are exempt from steep government import duties and are therefore affordable to the urban middle class. Suzuki makes and sells about 30,000 cars, vans, and trucks in Pakistan annually.

Other Japanese auto companies are also seeking to assemble cars in Pakistan, and Honda already participates in a joint venture producing over 18,000 motorcycles a year. Ford, Fiat, Massey-Ferguson, and a once Soviet firm called Belarus have arrangements similar to Suzuki's for the manufacture of tractors. Together these companies make about 40,000 tractors a year for domestic use, though that is not nearly enough for a nation with tens of millions of farmers.

Pakistan makes its own locomotives and railroad cars, as it has since the days of the British. In addition, the nation manufactures about half a million tires a year.

Industrial Workers

Less than 3 percent of the nation's labor force works in large factories, but these workers are the elite of Pakistani labor. Many of them belong to labor unions allied with specific political parties, and the unions have won them higher wages, longer vacations, and more holidays than most Pakistanis enjoy. A forklift operator at a chemical plant in

Karachi, for example, makes 1,700 rupees ($70) a month, and enjoys four weeks of vacation and sixteen holidays annually.

To avoid paying union-scale wages and benefits, many Pakistani companies hire workers for just a few months at a time. As temporary laborers, these workers are not covered by laws that give permanent employees the right to form unions.

Cottage Industry

More common than the large factory is the small workshop. Millions of Pakistanis work in small groups, making carpets, knives, furniture, hockey sticks, cricket bats, and leather goods such as bridles, saddles, and whips.

Carpets alone account for 5 percent of Pakistan's exports. They are made primarily by children nine to sixteen years of age, because they have the most nimble fingers. The young weavers work long hours in gloomy, dimly lit workshops, and often they cut their fingers or develop asthma. Pakistani carpets are among the finest in the world, but the boys and girls who make them earn only about 25 rupees (one dollar) a day. Most of the profits go to middlemen.

Middlemen also exploit adult women who work at home. About one third of Pakistani women living in towns and cities work four to eight hours a day at tasks in addition to their domestic duties. Many work as part-time servants, but the majority work at home, where they can keep flexible hours. They sew clothes, stitch shopping bags, weave baskets, roll cigarettes, and make lace and embroidery. Middlemen supply them with materials and pay them by the piece. Their rates are appallingly low. A woman who stitches a dozen pairs of cotton gloves, for example, earns just 4 rupees (16 cents) for her effort.

Recently, some women have formed cooperatives to eliminate the middleman. They buy their own material and sell their goods as a unit to large buyers. Such groups, however, are still unusual.

Labor Abroad

Next to cotton products, Pakistan's biggest export is its labor. Over 1 million Pakistanis work abroad, three fourths of them in the oil-rich nations of the Persian Gulf.

The men who leave their villages for the Middle East are usually young, single, and jobless. For several years they work long hours on docks, oil rigs, and construction sites, sleeping at night in crowded dormitories. They do it because they can earn eight times as much in the Persian Gulf as they can in Pakistan, if they could find jobs in Pakistan at all. When they return to Pakistan, tired and prosperous, the young men are more attractive to families seeking husbands for their daughters.

Pakistanis who work abroad send "remittances" home of almost $2 billion a year. This is below the peak levels of the early 1980's, but it still amounts to over 30 percent of Pakistan's foreign currency earnings, and almost 5 percent of the nation's gross national product.

What is unusual about these remittances is that for the first time in the history of Pakistan, wealth is flowing directly to ordinary people rather than to landlords, bankers, and army officers. The average Pakistani working abroad supports seven people back home, and there is enough money left over for families to buy some of the conveniences of modern life: air conditioners, refrigerators, sewing machines, color television sets, and videocassette players.

Even after a family has purchased these appliances, there is usually money left to invest in something that can generate income, such as land, a bank account, or a Suzuki truck.

When Iraq invaded Kuwait in August 1990, 67,000 Pakistanis returned home. But close to a million Pakistanis still live in the Middle East. The majority of them work in Saudi Arabia and the United Arab Emirates, the two nations that are also the biggest foreign investors in Pakistani businesses.

In addition, over 400,000 former Pakistanis are citizens of Britain, and at least 80,000 Pakistanis live in the United States. These emigrants are thriving as news vendors, restaurant owners, shopkeepers, and factory workers, and they too send money to poorer relatives back in Pakistan.

Heroin and Opium

As mentioned in Chapter IX, much of the heroin in the United States and Western Europe comes from Pakistan and Afghanistan. Along the borders of these two countries there are probably more than eighty laboratories refining heroin and opium. The illegal manufacture of these drugs is one of the largest industries in Pakistan, and the money it generates is deposited in banks throughout the nation. One of these banks, allegedly, is the notorious Bank of Credit and Commerce International. Some of the illegal drugs made in Pakistan are sent to Karachi, where there are several hundred thousand heroin addicts. But most of the drugs are delivered to fishermen on the remote Makran Coast of Baluchistan, and at night the fishermen quietly transport their cargo out to ships in international waters.

Corruption

Unfortunately, drug smuggling is only the most obvious symptom of widespread illegality in Pakistan. Throughout the nation, bribery is a common and accepted practice. Business executives must bribe civil servants to place license applications on the right desk, utility employees to keep electricity from being cut off, and railroad officials to deliver supplies on time. Few of the recipients regard their bribes as anything more than tips.

A vicious cycle is at work. Bribery is common because public employees are underpaid, for the government's revenues are small. Tax revenue is insufficient because tax collectors routinely take bribes to underreport a business's income. Indeed, about half of the taxable income in Pakistan is hidden from view. Even large items such as cars and refrigerators are typically paid for in cash so that nothing will be reported to the government. If there is a receipt for a purchase, the amount written down is almost always much lower than the amount actually paid. This is particularly true for exports; the unreported payments for exported goods are often deposited in foreign bank accounts.

One reason many Pakistanis feel free to conceal income from the government is that agricultural income is completely exempt from taxation. Almost all of the nation's tax burden falls on just 1 million businessmen and salaried workers. Understandably, they deeply resent paying high taxes when the largest landlords, who still comprise a large majority of the National Assembly, exempt themselves from paying any taxes at all. Many businessmen turn the injustice to their advantage. They buy land and disguise their taxable earnings as agricultural income.

Some of the worst examples of corruption in Pakistan are the many bad loans made by government-owned banks. After the banks were nationalized in the 1970's, some government officials abused their trust and loaned money to political allies, without requiring any collateral. Many of these loans have never been paid back, and the nation's banks have lost a great deal of money. Pakistan's new prime minister, Nawaz Sharif, is currently trying to sell several of the country's biggest banks, as well as many of its largest factories, back to private investors.

A more benign kind of illegality is the trade in foreign-made appliances. Refrigerators and other appliances that arrive in the port of Karachi are exempt from expensive Pakistani customs duties if they are bound for landlocked Afghanistan. But only the receipts actually make it to Afghanistan. The appliances themselves are sold in Pakistan on the black market—at prices middle-class Pakistanis can afford.

Energy

Pakistan is not self-sufficient in energy, and this is a big economic problem. Hydroelectric dams and natural-gas fields furnish much of Pakistan's energy needs, but the supply of hydroelectricity drops greatly during the dry winter months. Then oil-burning generators must

Engineers at the construction site of an electric power plant in the Korangi district of Karachi.   United Nations

provide the power. Over one fourth of Pakistan's energy comes from imported oil, and even when the price of oil is low, Pakistan's exports barely earn enough money to pay for it. When the price of oil climbs steeply, as it did briefly in 1990, the effect is a devastating increase in Pakistan's foreign debt.

Foreign Debt

Pakistan's debt to foreign nations is currently around $14 billion, equivalent to about one third of the country's gross national product. The debt continues to grow because Pakistan exports low-technology items such as cotton, cotton cloth, and carpets, while it imports more expensive high-technology items such as industrial equipment, motor vehicles, weapons, and also, of course, oil.

Each year the government of Pakistan spends well over a billion dollars, almost a quarter of its budget, paying interest on its foreign debt. Ironically, if the government could spend this money on education rather than on interest, Pakistan's young people might soon be skilled enough to make high-technology items themselves.

Difficulties Ahead

Pakistan's immediate economic future is uncertain. Kidnappings in Karachi are beginning to discourage foreign investment. Remittances from Pakistanis working in the Middle East have declined recently, and unfortunately Pakistan has no other cushion for difficult times. The government has cash and gold reserves to pay for just eight weeks of imports.

With 115 million hard-working people, Pakistan will survive its difficulties. But the standard of living of its people is unlikely to improve much in the early 1990's. Even assuming that the nation's economy can grow at the robust clip of 6 percent per year, as it has in the past, 3 percent of this increase will merely keep pace with population growth. Another 2 percent may be consumed by rising interest on a growing foreign debt, and by increases in the price of imported oil. Even if Pakistan enjoys some good harvests in the next few years, real economic growth is likely to be quite small.

Food

Pakistan is a poor nation with many problems, but its cuisine is one of the finest in the world. Perhaps only the French and Chinese have food as consistently delicious and rich as the food in Pakistan and India. The fare of many other nations is dull and bland by comparison.

Every day, in every city and village in Pakistan, illiterate women turn ordinary vegetables such as lentils, okra, squash, spinach, potatoes, onions, gourds, cauliflower, green beans, and even peas and carrots into delights that could please the most discriminating gourmet.

Spices

The key to Pakistani cooking is the use of dozens of spices, which even the poor can afford to buy. The spices are then blended a hundred different ways, so that even if the ingredients are the same from one day to

A shopkeeper selling dried fruit and nuts in Peshawar. Pakistan Directorate of Films and Publications

the next, the flavors will vary. In the West we use the word "curry" to describe Indian and Pakistani food, but the word is merely a British corruption of *turcarri*, the Hindi and Urdu word for "sauce." A Pakistani talks instead about specific spices, perhaps cautioning you that a particular chili pepper will be hot.

Although spices are sold in powdered form, they stay fresh for only a few weeks. A good cook (or her husband) must therefore make many trips to the shop of a spice merchant, who displays his wares in the open air, in baskets filled several feet high with pungent powders of vivid colors.

At home, a cook will select the spices she wants and grind them together with a little bit of water to make a paste. Then she will thoroughly brown the spices in *ghee* before adding them to vegetables or meat. *Ghee* is what is left of melted butter made from water-buffalo milk when the solid residue at the bottom is strained out. Because it can be heated to a much higher temperature than butter without burning, *ghee* is one of the core ingredients of Pakistani cooking.

Pakistani Dishes

The most common food in Pakistan is *dhal.* It is a side dish at almost every meal in Pakistan, and for poor people it often suffices as an entire meal. *Dhal* is made from orange and yellow lentils that are boiled and mixed with onions, pepper, garlic, turmeric, cinnamon, ginger, and perhaps also lemon, bay leaves, and chilies—until the liquid has the consistency of porridge. The lentils in *dhal* are the chief source of protein for those Pakistanis who can rarely afford meat.

Other popular vegetable dishes include *alu gobi*, potatoes and cauliflower with spices, *alu mattar*, potatoes and peas with spices, and *bhendi bhaji*, fried okra with spices.

Even landless villagers can usually afford to eat meat once every week or two. Pakistanis who live in cities, or in sheepherding areas such as the North-West Frontier Province or Baluchistan, often eat meat every other day, or even daily.

The Pakhtuns, however, use fewer spices than do Punjabis or Sindhis. Their favorite dish is *chapli kebab*, fried patties of ground mutton or lamb mixed with green onions, crushed pomegranate seeds, and salt. *Chapli kebab*s are as common in the North-West Frontier Province as hamburgers are in America, and they are popular throughout Pakistan.

Some Spices Used in Pakistani Cooking

ajowan	fennel	nutmeg
allspice	fenugreek	pepper
anise	garam masala	pomegranate seeds
bay leaves	(a common	poppy seeds
cardamom	mixture of spices)	rose water
chilies	garlic	saffron
cinnamon	ginger	tamarind
cloves	mace	tulsi
coriander	mint	turmeric
cumin	mustard	

Afghan refugees cooking a meal in the North-West Frontier Province. ICEF 9374/83/Pakistan—UNICEF Photo by N. Rehman

In Baluchistan, the nomads are so poor and villages are so remote that spices are hard to come by. The only thing they usually add to their lamb or mutton is salt.

Islam, unlike Hinduism, does not encourage its followers to be vegetarians, although it does forbid the eating of pork. Favorite meat dishes in Pakistan include *shami kebab*, small patties of minced lamb or beef mixed with onions, eggs, and many spices; *seekh kebab*, larger patties of minced lamb or beef mixed with chick-pea flour and spices, rolled into tubes and then grilled; mutton *korma*, cubes of mutton and fried onion in a thick, spicy gravy; and *saag gosht*, cubes of mutton or beef in a spicy spinach sauce.

Also highly popular is chicken barbecued in a variety of styles, including *tikka*, in which it is sliced into cubes and charcoal grilled, and *tandoor*, in which it is slit, stuffed with spices, and quickly cooked whole in a very hot oven.

Because Pakistani cooking is so full of rich, spicy sauces, side dishes tend to be light and cool. *Khira raita*, plain yogurt with cucumbers, lemon juice, and mint, is extremely common. So are yogurt-and-onion salad, and various chutneys made from mangoes, coconuts, mint leaves, and tamarind.

Bread

Most Pakistanis do not use knives and forks. Instead, they break off a piece of bread and, with the right hand, use it to scoop up meat or vegetables as if the bread were a fork. Westerners who try to eat this way will usually get the tips of their fingers greasy, but even a child in Pakistan always finishes a meal with clean fingers.

The three most common kinds of bread in Pakistan are *chapati*s, *paratha*s, and *naan*. A *chapati* is a flat one-foot-wide disc of unleav-

Women making chapatis *and* parathas *at a* tandoor *oven in Karachi.* U.N. Photo 153527/John Isaac

ened whole-meal bread cooked on both sides and then briefly held over a flame. It looks like a Mexican tortilla, but it is smoother.

*Paratha*s are similar to *chapati*s, but because oil is added during the kneading of the flour, parathas are softer, thicker and flakier than *chapati*s. They look like flour tortillas, and along with *chapati*s, they are a mainstay of the Pakistani diet. A basket stacked with either *chapati*s or *paratha*s is served at every meal in Pakistan—breakfast, lunch, and dinner—whether the home is rich or poor.

Most Pakistanis don't eat *naan* as often as they eat *chapati*s or *paratha*s, but among the Pakhtuns *naan* is the most common kind of bread. *Naan* is made from white flour, and it is kneaded with milk, yogurt, poppy seeds, and an egg mixed in. After the baking, a piece of *naan* is longer and thicker than a *chapati* or a *paratha*.

Traditionally, *chapati*s, *paratha*s, and *naan* are cooked in a *tandoor* oven. A *tandoor* can be made of clay, metal, or stone, and is often four to five feet deep and two to three feet wide. A small opening at the top of a curved oven is narrower than the oven itself, perhaps a foot and a half wide. When *chapati*s and *paratha*s bake in a *tandoor*, they stick vertically to the side of the oven. Then someone removes them with tongs and holds them briefly over a flame to make them puff out slightly.

Although *tandoor* ovens are found in homes and restaurants all over Pakistan, many Pakistanis today, probably a majority, prepare their bread in large frying pans instead.

Sweets

A Pakistani meal is not complete without dessert. Usually dessert will consist of fresh fruit such as oranges, mangoes, apricots, and a variety of melons, but often it will also include a prepared sweet. The sweets of Pakistan and India are wonderfully delicious, yet little known in the West.

Unlike Western desserts, Pakistani sweets are often made from fresh milk that has been boiled, curdled, and dried. In *ras gula*s, or cream cheese balls, for example, dried milk is mixed with sugar, cardamom pods, and a little bit of flour before it is cooked in hot syrup flavored with rose water. When the resulting sweet balls cool off, they are somewhat akin to *halvah*. *Ras gula*s are not only served as a dessert, but are also served occasionally at teatime, and quite often during holidays. Other sweets are made by combining dried milk and sugar with coconut, pistachios, pumpkin pulp, and even carrots.

A vendor selling sweets in the city of Hyderabad, in Sind. Mark Weston

A different kind of dessert is *kheer*, vermicelli noodles boiled in milk, with sugar, almond paste and pistachios added to make a cool and spicy pudding. Rice pudding is also common in Pakistan, even among the poor. Another pudding is *shahi tukra*, which is white bread fried and then soaked in milk flavored with cardamom and saffron.

A Full-Time Job

Shahi tukra, like many other Pakistani dishes, dates from the time of the Mughal emperors. The royal families loved to eat well and went to great lengths to find the best ingredients and the most imaginative chefs. Over centuries, as royal meals grew more varied and refined, knowledge of these dishes spread widely across the subcontinent. Ironically, one of the chief legacies of the luxury of the Mughal empire is that today even the poor in Pakistan enjoy some of the finest cooking on earth.

The preparation of a Pakistani meal, however, is often quite time-consuming. Leafing through recipes of Pakistani dishes, one finds phrases like, "marinate the chicken for eight to ten hours," or "simmer for two to three hours, stirring constantly."

For many in Pakistan, cooking is virtually a full-time job. The typical Pakistani family is an extended family, and one woman may cook for eight to ten people while another woman milks the water buffalo and does the laundry. Wealthy and upper-middle-class households will hire a servant, often a man, to do the cooking. He will also shop for groceries before meals and will wash the dishes afterward.

Most men in Pakistan, though, have very little to do with the preparation of a meal. They only know that at the end of the day a wife, mother, or servant will cook them a delicious dinner, their reward after a hard day in the fields, classroom, factory, or office.

Arts and Entertainment

The streets of Pakistan's cities and towns are alive with the vibrant culture of the nation. Buses hurry by with rainbow-colored calligraphy painted on their rear windows. Shopkeepers play tapes of their favorite singers, who sometimes sing verses from poems hundreds of years old. Giant billboards with pictures of voluptuous women and muscular men with machine guns advertise the latest movies. And often, looming above the horizon, there is a huge and magnificent mosque, centuries old, an architectural reminder to everyone of Pakistan's rich cultural heritage.

Architecture

The architecture of the Mughal Empire is the pride of Pakistan and one of the glories of human achievement. Mughal architects combined the Muslim preferences for large domes, slender towers, and pointed arch-

Calligraphy inside the Wazir Khan mosque in Lahore.   Pakistan Directorate of Films and Publications

ways with the Hindu use of red sandstone, white marble, and inlaid stones and jewels. Mughal artists decorated their monuments with verses from the Qur'an and intricate patterns of flowers made with stone, plaster, tile, and glass. Most of this calligraphy is in Arabic rather than Urdu, for Muslims revere Arabic as the language God chose when he revealed the Qur'an to Muhammad.

The most impressive building in Pakistan is the Badshahi mosque in Lahore, built during the reign of the pious Emperor Aurangzeb in the early 1670's. Beside three enormous onion-shaped domes of white marble, and surrounded by giant walls of red sandstone, is a courtyard that sometimes holds over 100,000 worshippers, making the Badshahi mosque the second largest mosque in the world. The largest mosque, also in Pakistan, is the Faisal mosque in Islamabad, constructed in the early 1980's as a gift from Saudi Arabia.

The Badshahi mosque is part of the Lahore Fort. A sprawling complex of fortified walls and open-air pavilions, it was built during the reigns of four Mughal emperors between the 1580's and 1670's. Perhaps the most spectacular pavilion there is the Shish Mahal (Palace of Mirrors), designed for Shah Jahan's queen, Mumtaz Mahal, in the early 1630's. During the heat of the day the palace is naturally air-conditioned, for marble screens cool the air as it blows through. At night, thousands of tiny mirrors placed in the walls and ceilings reflect candlelight, twinkling like stars.

The view of the Badshahi mosque from the Lahore Fort is a panorama of Mughal architecture. Pakistan Directorate of Films and Publications

Craftsmen painting tiles and pottery at a kiln in Multan.   Pakistan Directorate of Films and Publications

Just outside of Lahore are the Shalimar Gardens, built for Shah Jahan in 1642. This onetime playground for the royal family contains terraced lawns, pools, waterfalls, and over 400 fountains.

In Sind, architects have favored the use of blue and white tile rather than sandstone. Probably the two greatest monuments in Sind are the Shah Jahan mosque in Thatta, a masterpiece of intricate brick and tilework constructed in the late 1640's, and the tomb of the great Sindhi poet Shah Abdul Latif, erected at Bhitshah, near Hyderabad, in the mid-1750's.

Painting

The era of the Mughals is known for its miniature paintings as well as its grand architecture. With brushes made from just one hair of a squirrel's tail or a single cat's whisker, the Persians of the sixteenth century produced paintings of exquisite detail. Indian artists quickly absorbed their style and produced hundreds of miniature paintings themselves. Many of these paintings are among the finest examples of miniatures in the world. They show us secular scenes such as court ceremonies, royal hunts, armies in battle, and harem life. There are no religious scenes among the miniatures, however, for Muslims abhor any portrayal of the face of God, Muhammad, or a Muslim saint as the making of a graven image.

The Mughal legacy of painting in detail continues today in a rougher form in a most unlikely place: the sides of trucks. Nearly every truck in Pakistan is as brightly and intricately decorated as a circus wagon, with artists painting everything on them from the Taj Mahal to a snow-capped mountain to an F-16 fighter jet.

The rear windows of buses are also decorated with brightly colored calligraphy, usually in Urdu. Sometimes the calligraphy is a verse from the Qur'an. More often it is an amusing message such as "Naturally Air-Conditioned," or just a description of the bus route.

Modern painters whom Pakistanis admire include Abdur Rahman Chughtai (1897–1975), who carried on the tradition of miniature painting, and Sadequain (1930–1986), a mural painter and a master at Qur'anic calligraphy.

An intricately painted truck north of Islamabad.   Mark Weston

Poetry

Unlike Americans, large numbers of Pakistanis adore poetry and often memorize long poems. A *mushaira* (poetry reading) in Pakistan can sometimes attract thousands of listeners. The man who is probably the most widely admired poet of the Urdu language, Ghalib (1797–1869), wrote many of his best poems while still a teenager. When he was twenty, he stopped writing in Urdu and wrote instead in Persian, which in the nineteenth century was still the language of the subcontinent's most educated Muslims.

In the Urdu language, Ghalib is most famous for his *ghazal*s. The *ghazal* is the most popular form of Urdu and Persian poetry. It has five or more two-line couplets in which all the second lines rhyme with each other: aa, ba, ca, da, ea.

Many *ghazal*s describe the joys and pain of unrequited love, or the love of humanity for God, but a *ghazal* can convey any human emotion. Ghazals are still sung today by popular singers and recited by ordinary people. Here is one couplet by Ghalib:

> *Passion feels confined*
> *even in the heart—*
> *the sea's restless surge*
> *absorbed in a pearl.*[1]

The national poet of modern Pakistan is Sir Muhammad Iqbal (1877–1938), widely known in Pakistan as the "Allama" (the "Wise"). Iqbal wrote poetry in Urdu and Persian and gave lectures in English, always seeking to rekindle the spirit of Muslim brotherhood in the modern world. In his greatest collection of poetry, *Bal-e-Jibril* (*Gabriel's Wing*), published in 1936, Iqbal asked young Muslims to renounce Western materialism, on the one hand, and Eastern mysticism, on the other. Only men of both faith and action, he wrote, could strengthen Islam and change the world.

> *If a Muslim is without faith, he is a slave to destiny,*
> *Endowed with faith, he becomes the destiny of God.*[2]

Iqbal has sometimes been compared to John Milton, the seventeenth-century Puritan author of *Paradise Lost*. Like Milton, Iqbal was not only a great poet whose themes were primarily religious, but he was also active in the politics of his time. In 1930, Iqbal called for a

[1] Translation by Frances W. Pritchett, Associate Professor of Modern Indic Languages, Columbia University, from a work in progress.

[2] Nadwi, Syed Abul Hasan Ali. *Glory of Iqbal*, translated from Urdu by Muhammad Asif Kidwai. Karachi: Haqji Arfeen Academy, 1972, 1987, p. 96.

separate Muslim state in northwest India, the first man of stature ever to do so. Eight years later he helped persuade Muhammad Ali Jinnah of the necessity for the establishment of Pakistan. For this reason Pakistanis regard Muhammad Iqbal as the spiritual father of their nation, and he is buried at the Lahore Fort, just next to the Badshahi mosque.

Many Pakistani intellectuals greatly admire Iqbal, but others prefer the poetry of Faiz Ahmed Faiz (1911–1984). Faiz was a socialist, and much of his poetry concerns class struggle. His work was banned from Pakistani television and radio during the eras of military government, but his best romantic poetry is enjoyed by millions.

> *Ah, those fortunate people*
> *who considered their life work to be love,*
> *and those who were in love with work.*
> *I kept busy all my life;*
> *I made some love, I did some work.*
> *Work kept interfering with love;*
> *love got in the way of work.*
> *At last I got sick of it all*
> *and left both half-finished.*[3]

The best-loved poet of the Sindhi language is Shah Abdul Latif (1689–1752), a Sufi mystic who wrote about love and the Sindhi countryside. Latif's poetry is still widely recited in Sind today, by illiterate farmers as well as university professors.

Probably the most famous poet of the Pashto language is Khushal Khan Khattak (1613–1689), who died the year Shah Abdul Latif was born. Khattak was a Pakhtun chief who spent years fighting and fleeing

[3]Lazard, Naomi, translator. *The True Subject: Selected Poems of Faiz Ahmed Faiz.* Copyright 1987 by Princeton University Press. Poem, "I Made Some Love, I Did Some Work," reprinted by permission of Princeton University Press.

the armies of the Mughal emperor Aurangzeb. He wrote vivid and wise poetry about war, honor, and the art of government. He also wrote poems describing the beauty of women and nature, often using military metaphors:

> *The tulips are as bright as flashes from the huntsmen's guns.*
> *The roses stand, a warrior phalanx, spears by their sides.*[4]

Music

In the thirteenth century a poet and musician named Amir Khusrau composed some of the earliest *raga*s, the traditional rhythmic form of Indian classical music. He also began an Indian Muslim tradition of having musicians at a royal court. Over the next several centuries some of these Muslim musicians invented the *sitar* and the *tabla*, the long, stringed instrument and the small pair of hand drums that now epitomize the music of the South Asian subcontinent. Even today, most of the performers of traditional music in north India are Muslims, not Hindus.

The majority of Pakistanis, however, prefer popular songs to classical music. These songs are written for romantic movie musicals. When a film is released, its songs are broadcast over the radio and heard by tens of millions of Pakistanis.

Songs from Indian movies are especially popular in Pakistan; most Pakistanis understand Hindi with ease, since it is almost identical to spoken Urdu. Even in remote villages, when Pakistanis play cassette tapes they often listen to songs from Indian, not Pakistani, movies.

---

[4]Spain, James W. *The Way of the Pathans.* Karachi: Oxford University Press, 1962, 1972, p. 109.

Many Pakistanis feel that songs from Indian movies have catchier melodies and snappier lyrics than do songs from Pakistani films. The reason for the disparity between Indian and Pakistani songs is probably simply that the artistic community in Bombay, the filmmaking center of India, is larger and therefore livelier than the one in Lahore, the cultural center of Pakistan.

Not all of Pakistan's popular music comes from films. Folk songs in regional languages such as Punjabi, Sindhi, and Pashto are also popular, especially in villages. Each of these languages has a rich oral tradition of songs and poems. In Pashto, the language of the Pakhtuns, many ballads are about honor and revenge. In Punjabi and Sindhi, songs are more often about tragic young couples with fates similar to that of Romeo and Juliet. The sorrowful tales of Sohni and Mahinwal, and of Heer and Ranjha, are still widely sung today.

Folk songs are commonly broadcast by rural radio stations. Typically, a folk group consists of one or two singers and several musicians playing the harmonium and the *dholaq*, instruments akin to a low-octave accordion and a barrel drum.

One form of Punjabi dance music, called *bhangra*, has such a driving beat that it has become popular with the children of Indian and Pakistani emigrants living in London. Another style of music, *qawwali*, is devotional in nature. *Qawwali* is often performed at Sufi shrines on Thursday night, the night before the Muslim sabbath.

Movies

Pakistan's film industry has always been tiny, for in 1947 most of the Muslims in India's film industry elected to stay in Bombay rather than move to Lahore. Today, Pakistan produces only about eighty feature-length movies a year.

Nearly all Pakistani movies are long, melodramatic love stories with

Movie advertisements in an Urdu-language newspaper from Lahore.

plenty of singing, although recently there have been some films about guns, gangs, and smuggling. There is no kissing or hand-holding in Pakistani movies. When two people are about to kiss, there may suddenly be a scene of snow-capped mountains or vast fields of flowers.

Except in Karachi, movie theaters are shrinking in number, their function replaced by videocassette players in city living rooms and village teahouses. But many poor people still go to the movies, because tickets are cheap and most theaters are air conditioned. For the poor, movie theaters are often the only escape from heat and humidity.

As with popular music, Pakistanis generally prefer Indian films to those from their own nation. This is mainly because the small studios in Pakistan cannot match the big budgets that Indian studios routinely spend on their films. But it is also because under military governments the censorship in Pakistan has been much tighter than censorship in India. By Pakistani law, films are unsuitable for exhibition if they undermine Islam, malign Pakistan or its traditions, or contain vulgarity.

The Zia government banned theaters from showing Indian films because of their scenes of hand-holding and hugging, and until 1980 few Pakistanis had any opportunity to see Indian movies. But since the early 1980's videocassettes of Indian films have been widely and openly smuggled into Pakistan, and have been enjoyed by millions.

The popularity of Indian movies makes it more difficult for many Pakistani films to make money, but small-budget films in regional languages, especially in Punjabi, continue to thrive.

Television and Video

In most of Pakistan there is only one television channel, and it is run by the government. For about eleven hours a day it broadcasts dramas, religious discussions and instruction, news and important speeches, a morning children's hour, a religious quiz show, squash, cricket, and field hockey tournaments, live concerts of regional music, and a few programs from the United States such as *Full House* and *Kojak.* Each evening there is an hour of news. A woman reads the news for half an hour in Urdu, then another woman reads it for a half an hour in English. The evening news is mainly a headline service, and under some governments it has been quite biased. Many Pakistanis get their news instead from Urdu-language radio broadcasts by the BBC (British Broadcasting Corporation).

Although there is little live theater in Pakistan, the prime-time dramas on Pakistani television are interesting and well written, and often deal with serious issues. The programs are popular not only in Pakistan, but also in those areas of India within range of Pakistani TV signals. Conversely, residents of Lahore often watch Indian movies broadcast from the nearby city of Amritsar.

In addition, Muslim clerics discuss a wide variety of religious topics on television for an hour or more each evening.

Because there was only one television channel in Pakistan throughout the 1980's, Pakistanis embraced the video revolution, which allowed them to see Indian movies. Most urban middle-class families purchased videocassette players, and today there are video rental shops in almost every neighborhood of every city in Pakistan. The importation of videocassettes is illegal, but shop owners usually bribe local policemen to keep their stores open.

Most movie videos are recorded illegally—pirated by technicians in the United Arab Emirates from satellite transmissions around the globe. Even so, video stores in Pakistan are amply stocked with a large selection of Indian and American movies, and sometimes even with pornography. Most Pakistanis prefer Indian movies because they enjoy the songs, and because Hindi is easier for them to understand than English. Young and educated Pakistanis, however, may watch several American movies a week.

In May 1990 a new television company began broadcasting news from Ted Turner's Cable News Network (CNN) to the cities of Karachi, Islamabad, and Rawalpindi, and in May 1991 to Lahore as well. Anyone in these cities with a television set can watch CNN; no special dishes or antennas are necessary.

The decision to begin this second television channel was made by Benazir Bhutto. It may prove to be the most significant action of her brief administration, because the channel is opening more of the world to English-speaking Pakistanis. They have been fascinated by the intensity of political debate in the United States, and by live coverage of events such as a U.S. Senate committee vigorously questioning the Secretary of Defense.

Because Pakistan's government has been slow to allow new television channels, and because government-controlled news programs and conservative Muslim clerics dominate so much of the national network's programming, Pakistanis spend many hours watching and listening to foreign news reports and viewing foreign movies on videocassettes. Ironically, the refusal of government officials and Muslim theologians to share television time with other Pakistanis has resulted in a loss of their influence, and a large transfer of cultural power to non-Muslim sources: the newsrooms of CNN and the BBC, and the movie studios of Bombay and Hollywood.

Education,
Democracy, and
the Future

More than forty years after independence, Pakistan continues to have one of the lowest literacy rates in the world. Only about 35 percent of Pakistani men and 15 percent of Pakistani women can read and write. In rural areas the literacy rate for women is about 7 percent. Unfortunately, these appalling statistics will not improve soon. According to the World Bank, barely a third of Pakistan's children finish the fifth grade.

Other nations as poor as Pakistan, such as China and Sri Lanka, have literacy rates over 80 percent. Pakistan lags behind for two reasons. First, almost half of its national budget goes to the military, while only about 9 percent is spent on education. This is a much smaller percentage than the 12 to 15 percent spent in most Asian nations.

A young girl learning to write in Karachi.   U.N. Photo 152390/John Isaac

Second, Pakistan's enormous birthrate makes it almost impossible to raise the literacy rate. The number of schools in Pakistan has doubled in the last twenty-five years, but the population has too. There are twice as many illiterate people in Pakistan today as there were a generation ago. The percentage of people who can read and write, which was 22 percent in 1972, has hardly increased at all. Because illiterate women rarely use birth control, population growth will not slow down until literacy rises. The twin plagues of illiteracy and high population growth thus directly reinforce each other.

Elementary Schools

Most villages and most urban neighborhoods have free elementary schools, but classrooms at these schools are crowded and quite bare. Most have only benches, an open window with no glass, a blackboard, and perhaps a ceiling fan and a map. If a class is particularly crowded, students may sit tightly packed on straw mats on the ground. In some rural areas, classes are held outdoors, for many villages have no school building.

In towns and cities nearly every boy and girl begins the first grade at age five, and even in rural areas almost 90 percent of the boys and over

Children at an outdoor class in the town of Balakot, in the North-West Frontier Province.   United Nations/Wolff

30 percent of the girls start school. Pens and paper are expensive for most Pakistanis, so students commonly carry chalk to class, along with a small piece of slate fastened inside a wooden frame. Elementary school teachers prepare their students to read, write, and do simple arithmetic, and in the countryside they teach some basic principles of farm management and food preservation. When students address a teacher, they stand up, and each day begins with a prayer.

Most students also spend some time each week reading the Qur'an after school. Girls commonly read it in the home of a relative or a neighbor, while boys more often read the Qur'an at a local mosque. They read phrases in the original Arabic script, usually without any translation into their local language. Nonetheless, many students learn long passages of the Qur'an by heart, and a few even memorize the entire book. In the 1980's, General Zia encouraged thousands of mosques to function also as elementary schools, usually with coed classes for the first three grades.

Unfortunately, less than half of Pakistani city children finish eighth grade. In rural areas the percentage of boys in school at age fourteen is just 7 percent, and for girls it is less than 1 percent.

Why Students Leave School

For boys, the primary reason for leaving is the lack of schools beyond the fifth grade. Few villages have middle schools, and transportation from one village to the next is difficult. Even in cities, the cost of buying books and uniforms for a child in middle school is often more than a poor family can afford.

Girls leave school for different reasons. One is that they are needed at home to take care of younger children or to help with chores such as fetching water and milking water buffaloes. Another important reason girls drop out, or never attend school at all, is that 90 percent of the

Percentage of Pakistani Students in School in 1985

Age	Urban Boys	Urban Girls	Rural Boys	Rural Girls	Total
5	97.3%	88.6%	87.2%	30.7%	67.4%
9	61.2%	47.1%	45.1%	13.3%	36.5%
12	56.0%	35.5%	18.1%	2.9%	19.8%
14	52.5%	23.6%	7.2%	0.7%	13.8%

Source: *Women in Pakistan: An Economic and Social Strategy*, The World Bank, Washington, D.C., 1989, p. 114, Table 1B.

elementary schools in Pakistan have sanitation facilities with little or no privacy. Families often accept this fact and send girls to school anyway when they are six or seven years old, but as they approach puberty, the need for modesty makes it impossible for most girls to continue to go to school.

Similarly, even though schools are segregated by sex from the fourth grade onward, a family may not consider it proper to send a girl to a school if all of the teachers are male, as is often the case. The tragedy is that most Pakistani families today would gladly send a daughter to school if they felt they could do so without jeopardizing her respectability. But too few schools have female teachers and proper sanitation, and those that do are often far from home.

Even in urban areas three out of four girls drop out of school by age fourteen. This almost guarantees that twenty years from now there will be a new shortage of female teachers, causing yet another generation of girls to leave school.

Secondary Schools

When students are fourteen, they take a matriculation exam. Students who pass the exam begin high school, although Pakistanis sometimes call it "college." Roughly 50 percent of urban boys, 25 percent of urban girls and 7 percent of rural boys begin high school, but only about half of the students finish. Many teenage girls get married, and many teenage boys enter the working world.

Every day except Friday, the Muslim sabbath, students arrive at high school at around seven in the morning and attend seven or eight

Afghan refugees taking notes in a classroom outside Peshawar.   UNICEF 2935/88/John Isaac

classes during the day. At one thirty or two in the afternoon, students return home to eat lunch and take a nap. Thursday is a half day.

Classes include mathematics, two sciences, English, Urdu, Pakistani studies, and also Islamic studies. This course, made compulsory by General Zia, consists mainly of the reading of verses from the Qur'an. Depending on the school, an additional course may be available in English literature, economics, or a language such as Sindhi or Arabic.

In most public schools today, all classes are taught in Urdu except for foreign-language courses, such as English and Arabic. The language that teachers use in public middle and high schools has switched between Urdu and English four times over the last twenty years, to the great confusion and detriment of students and teachers. The unresolved conflict is that while the use of Urdu promotes national unity and pride, the use of English better prepares students for the world.

Because the standard of English teaching in public schools has declined in the last few years, there is a huge demand for private, English-speaking schools. Fees there are twenty to thirty times higher than fees at public schools, but landowners and businessmen readily pay them to ensure that their children learn to speak proper English. In these private schools, all courses are taught in English except Urdu and Islamic studies.

Throughout Pakistan the army runs "cantonment" schools for the sons and daughters of its officers. They are usually the best schools in rural areas, so local landlords and merchants often pay high fees for their children to attend the army schools too.

Wherever young Pakistanis go to school, they spend long hours studying English. Because English is so different from Urdu, it is a much harder language for Pakistanis to learn than French or Spanish is for an American. Even so, hundreds of thousands of students learn to speak English flawlessly.

Universities

Less than 3 percent of Pakistani men and less than 1 percent of Pakistani women receive a university education. This is mainly because in all of Pakistan there are only 22 universities and about a hundred small colleges of law, medicine, engineering, and agriculture.

The richest or best students study in Britain and the United States, for university students in Pakistan must be content with underpaid professors, small libraries, and a scarcity of scientific equipment. More ominously, several universities in Karachi have become so politicized by the ethnic strife between Sindhis and Mohajirs that students sometimes fight each other with guns and hand grenades.

In contrast to classes in secondary schools, university classes in Pakistan are coed. Nearly all university students are from cities and towns, and the few students who are from villages usually take jobs in cities after they graduate. It is rare in Pakistan to find a university graduate—a doctor, for instance—living in a village.

The Need to Make Education a Priority

If Pakistan is to join the ranks of industrialized nations, it will have to make education its first priority, as Japan did in the late nineteenth century, and as Taiwan and South Korea did in the early twentieth century. Even doubling the number of students and teachers in the next two decades will not be enough, for that can only match the growth in population. Pakistan must triple or, even better, quadruple the number of people in school.

Local communities desperately need money to lure female teachers to rural areas, to construct sanitation facilities on school grounds, to build middle schools in villages, and to buy more books. There is also a huge need for correspondence courses for the many young people who work as farm laborers and cannot leave home. But these things can be accomplished only if there is a massive change in national priorities.

Ideally, Pakistan's military leaders would welcome a transfer of funds to education. The sacrifice of several army divisions and airforce fighter jets today could help create a better-educated workforce and a more industrialized nation tomorrow, and in turn this would make Pakistan far more militarily powerful than it is at present. But it is a rare official who supports the reduction of his own budget, and Pakistan's defense expenditures will not shrink soon, because decisions as to the size of the defense budget are made by the military itself.

How Democratic Is Pakistan?

Civilian authority is weak in Pakistan. Generals ruled the nation for twenty-four of the thirty years between 1958 and 1988. Since then, the knowledge that Pakistan's top officers can return to power whenever they want has kept civilian prime ministers from challenging the military on major defense issues.

Pakistan's civilian leaders today enjoy only half of the fruits of democracy: They control only half of the total budget. A big question in Pakistan's political future is whether the military will ever allow full democracy to work. Will army officers not only allow democratically elected politicians to stay in office, but actually submit to their authority? This is an especially important issue in a nation with nuclear weapons.

Even if civilians do regain control over the military, they will have won just part of the battle for real democracy. A government's power is only as great as its ability to tax, and in Pakistan the tax base is quite small. Landlords pay no taxes and businessmen vastly underreport their income. Unlike most democracies, Pakistan does not have a true system of graduated income taxation where the rich pay a higher percentage of their income in taxes than the poor. Instead, just one million wage earners, and entrepreneurs paying customs duties, pay the bulk of Pakistan's taxes.

Voters in Pakistan often choose landlords and local businessmen to represent them in legislatures because they believe, correctly, that the more wealthy and powerful their representative is, the more likely he is to provide their local district with roads, schools, electricity, health clinics, and clean water. But if Pakistan's tax base were widened and the rich paid more taxes, then more money would be available for community projects, and ordinary citizens could be less dependent on their landlords and employers.

The wealthy men in Pakistan's legislatures will not vote to widen the tax base and raise their own taxes until the voters demand it of them, but at this time the question of taxation is not a burning issue. The government's tax receipts remain insufficient, and civil servants and policemen are severely underpaid. Often, officials earning low salaries are tempted to take bribes, and this corrupts the government and makes it responsive to the rich instead of to the poor.

Population Growth

Compounding nearly all of Pakistan's interconnected problems is the nation's high rate of population growth. If it continues increasing at the rate of 3 percent per year, Pakistan's population will double in twenty-five years, and will total 260 million people by the year 2020. Although the nation's farmers can feed that many people if more land is irrigated, such monstrous growth would negate nearly all of the country's economic gains and greatly fill already overcrowded cities with millions of new residents.

The birthrate will not fall without changes in family patterns. At present, a Pakistani couple needs to have six or seven children to ensure that two sons will grow up and support them in their old age. But as more money is spent on rural sanitation and water projects, perhaps the rate of infant mortality can be reduced enough for a family to feel secure having just four or five children. Even a slight reduction in the birthrate would produce enormous economic gains for the nation.

Women who work outside the home tend to have small families, but only a minority of Pakistani women pursue careers outside the home. The typical husband in Pakistan may not keep his wife in *purdah*, but he is still uncomfortable with the thought of his wife meeting men away from home. This attitude is changing, but the career woman with just one or two children will remain an exception in Pakistan for quite a while.

Perhaps the best that can be hoped for is a reduction of Pakistan's population growth to just under 2 percent per year. Even at this rate, the United Nations projects that there will be 213 million Pakistanis by the year 2025. By then there may be 1.6 billion people on the South Asian subcontinent, with roughly half of them illiterate.

A Vision of Peace

Can a nuclear-armed Pakistan remain at peace with a nuclear-armed India if both nations are bulging at the seams? Probably, but it would be easier if the two nations could come to an agreement on the status of Kashmir. Were it not for this tragic and ongoing dispute, India and Pakistan could even be allies. The two nations have much in common. When the subcontinent was partitioned in 1947, it was Muhammad Ali Jinnah's dream that the border between India and Pakistan be open and undefended, and that defense expenditures would occupy only a small portion of Pakistan's budget. Perhaps one day this dream will come true, and money for defense will be spent instead on education, health, and other pressing needs.

Pakistan has enormous problems, but it also has many strengths, and these, too, will last long into the future. From the Himalayan mountains to the Arabian Sea, for decades to come, Pakistan will continue to have some of the most magnificent architecture, lively streets, hardworking people, delicious food, loving families, and generous hosts in the world.

Bibliography

General Books on Pakistan

Duncan, Emma. *Breaking the Curfew: A Political Journey Through Pakistan*. London: Michael Joseph, 1989.

An anecdotal but thorough book on the people who run Pakistan: soldiers, businessmen, landlords, tribal chiefs, clerics, etc.

Nyrop, Richard F., editor. *Pakistan: A Country Study* (Area Handbook Series). Washington, D.C.: U.S. Government Printing Office, 1984.

An excellent reference book, comprehensive and readable.

Osborne, Christine. *An Insight and Guide to Pakistan*. Harlow, Essex, and New York: Longman House, 1983.

A well-written travel guide to the land, food, and tourist attractions of every region of Pakistan.

Quraeshi, Samina. *Legacy of the Indus*. New York: John Weatherhill, Inc., 1974.

A descriptive and beautifully written book on the people and daily life in different regions of Pakistan.

Reeves, Richard. *Passage to Peshawar*. New York: Simon and Schuster, 1984.

A good overview of life and politics in Pakistan.

Singhal, Damodar P. *Pakistan*. Englewood Cliffs, N.J.: Prentice-Hall, 1972.

A good one-volume history of Muslim India, and of Pakistan's first quarter of a century.

Taylor, David, compiler. *Pakistan* (World Bibliographical Series). Oxford, England, and Santa Barbara, Cal.: Clio Press, 1990.

Brief, easy-to-read descriptions of 797 books and articles on Pakistan. An excellent place to start for anyone doing research on the country.

Wilber, Donald M. *Pakistan—Its People, Its Society, Its Culture*. New Haven, Conn.: Hraf Press, 1964.

The most comprehensive one-volume book on Pakistan when it was published. Although out of date, it still provides a good introduction to Pakistan's languages, customs, and culture.

Wolpert, Stanley. *A New History of India*. New York: Oxford University Press, 1989.

Perhaps the best one-volume history of the South Asian subcontinent, although its coverage of Pakistan since independence is brief.

Chapter II:
The Land

The books by Richard F. Nyrop and Christine Osborne, listed above, were valuable sources for this chapter. Other useful books include:

Kureshy, K. U. *Geography of Pakistan*. Lahore: National Book Service, 1988.

A concise textbook on the terrain and economy of Pakistan.

Oxford Atlas for Pakistan. Karachi: Oxford University Press, 1988.

A paperback with a wide variety of maps of Pakistan.

Chapter III:
The People and Their Languages

The books by Samina Quraeshi, Richard F. Nyrop, and Emma Duncan, listed previously, were particularly helpful on this topic. Other valuable works include:

Abdullah, Ahmed. *The Historical Background of Pakistan and Its People*. Karachi: Tanzeem Publishers, 1973.

A scholarly study of Pakistan's linguistic groups.

Ahmed, Akbar S. *Pakistan Society—Islam, Ethnicity and Leadership in South Asia.* Karachi: Oxford University Press, 1986.

Thoughtful essays about various tribal groups in rural Pakistan.

Spain, James W. *The Way of the Pathans.* Karachi: Oxford University Press, 1962, 1972.

A sympathetic and entertaining portrait of the Pakhtun people.

Chapter IV:
Early History

Stanley Wolpert's book, listed previously, contains a concise account of Pakistan's early history. Other helpful books include:

Hawkes, Jacquetta. *The First Great Civilizations.* New York: Knopf, 1973.

This book contains a short but comprehensive chapter on the Indus River civilization.

Mahmud, S. F. *A Concise History of Indo-Pakistan.* Karachi: Oxford University Press, 1988.

A dry outline, but excellent for names, dates, and events.

Wheeler, R. E. Mortimer. *Five Thousand Years of Pakistan: An Archaeological Outline.* London: Christopher Johnson Ltd., 1950.

In this book Wheeler discusses the initial Muslim conquests of India, as well as the ancient Indus River cities.

————. *The Indus Civilization.* Cambridge, England: Cambridge University Press, 1953.

A vivid description by one of Britain's leading archeologists.

Chapter V:
The Mughal Empire

Gascoigne, Bamber. *The Great Moguls.* New York: Harper & Row, 1971.

A vivid description of a fabulous empire.

Hansen, Waldemar. *The Peacock Throne.* New York: Holt, Rinehart and Winston, 1972.

A gripping portrait of the Mughals.

Patnaik, Naveen. *A Second Paradise: Indian Courtly Life 1590–1947.* Garden City, N.Y.: Doubleday, 1985.

An excellent book detailing the splendor and luxury enjoyed by Indian nobility.

Chapters VI and VII:
British Rule,
The Birth of Pakistan

Akbar, M. J. *Nehru: The Making of India*. London: Viking, 1988.
> A useful book for understanding the negative view of Jinnah.

Ali, Chaudhri Muhammad. *The Emergence of Pakistan*. New York: Columbia University Press, 1967.
> An excellent book giving the Pakistani view of the years before and after independence, by a man who was briefly Prime Minister of Pakistan in 1955–1956.

Collins, Larry, and Dominique LaPierre. *Freedom at Midnight*. New York: Simon & Schuster, 1975.
> An easy-to-read book about the months leading up to the independence of India and Pakistan.

Fischer, Louis. *The Life of Mahatma Gandhi*. New York: Collier Books, 1950, 1962.
> A good book for its account of conversations between Gandhi and Jinnah, and between Jinnah and Lord Mountbatten.

Moorhouse, Geoffrey. *India Britannica*. New York: Harper & Row, 1983.
> A concise, and favorable, view of the British colonial era.

Wolpert, Stanley. *Jinnah of Pakistan*. New York: Oxford University Press, 1984.
> The definitive biography of the founder of Pakistan. (General Zia banned this book because it mentioned that Jinnah sometimes ate ham sandwiches, a food forbidden to Muslims.)

Chapter VIII:
The Loss of Democracy,
The Loss of East Pakistan

The books by Damodar Singhal and Richard F. Nyrop, listed previously, were valuable sources for this chapter. Other useful books include:

Keesing's Research Report. *Pakistan From 1947 to the Creation of Bangladesh*. New York: Scribner's, 1973.
> A good book for names, dates, and events.

Papanek, Gustav F. *Pakistan's Development*. Cambridge, Mass.: Harvard University Press, 1967.
> A good book on Pakistan's economic problems and growth during the years after independence.

Sisson, Richard, and Leo E. Rose. *War and Secession: Pakistan, India, and the*

Creation of Bangladesh. Berkeley, Cal.: University of California Press, 1990.
   An excellent new history of the secession of East Pakistan.
Ziring, Lawrence. *The Ayub Khan Era*. Syracuse, N.Y.: Syracuse University Press, 1971.
   A dry but thorough account of Ayub Khan's rule.

Chapter IX:
Pakistan Since 1971

The books by Emma Duncan, Richard Reeves, and Richard F. Nyrop, listed previously, are excellent sources on the recent history of Pakistan. So are articles from *The New York Times*, *Far Eastern Economic Review*, and *The Friday Times* of Lahore, currently Pakistan's liveliest English-language newspaper. Other helpful books include:
Akbar, M. J. *Kashmir: Behind the Vale*. New Delhi: Viking (Penguin Books India), 1991.
   A detailed and up-to-date history of Kashmir from an Indian point of view.
Bhutto, Benazir. *Daughter of Destiny*. New York: Simon and Schuster, 1989.
   Benazir Bhutto's autobiography. Biased, but basically accurate. In Pakistan this book is entitled *Daughter of the East*.
Burki, Shahid Javed. *Pakistan: A Nation in the Making*. Boulder, Colo.: Westview Press, 1986.
   A free-market–oriented view of Pakistan's recent history.
Lamb, Christina. *Waiting for Allah—Pakistan's Struggle for Democracy*. London: Hamish Hamilton, 1991.
   A correspondent for *The Financial Times* covers the rise and fall of Benazir Bhutto.
Spector, Leonard S. *The Undeclared Bomb*. Cambridge, Mass.: Ballinger Publishing Company, 1988.
   This book by the world's leading authority on nuclear proliferation has a long chapter on Pakistan's nuclear program.

Chapter X:
Daily Life

For this chapter I am indebted to the many Pakistanis who were my hosts or who took time out of their day to tell me how they live. Samina Quraeshi's book, listed previously, contains vivid portraits of daily life in rural Pakistan, while the book listed in the "Islam and Family" chapter below, *Women of Pakistan* by Khawar

Mumtaz and Farida Shaheed, discusses in detail the hard lives of rural women. Other useful books include:

Amin, Mohamed; Duncan Willets; and Brian Tetley. *Karachi*. Karachi: Pak American Commercial Ltd., 1986.

A beautifully photographed book about daily life in Pakistan's largest city.

Hafeez, Sabeeha. *The Metropolitan Women of Pakistan: Studies*. Karachi: Royal Book Company, 1981.

Six studies of middle-class and slum-dwelling women in Karachi.

Zameenzad, Adam. *The 13th House*. New York: Random House, 1987.

A well-written novel portraying daily life in a lower-middle-class home in Karachi.

Chapter XI:
Islam and Family

The books by Samina Quraeshi, Richard F. Nyrop, and Richard Reeves, listed previously, were useful sources for this chapter. Other helpful books include:

Ahmad, Aziz. *An Intellectual History of Islam in India*. Edinburgh: Edinburgh University Press, 1969.

A survey of the literature, arts, Sufi orders, and other subgroups of South Asian Islam.

Mumtaz, Khawar, and Farida Shaheed. *Women of Pakistan: Two Steps Forward, One Step Back?* Lahore: Vanguard Books, 1987.

A short but extraordinary book explaining the many problems Pakistani women face, both from longstanding customs and recent government policies.

The Qur'an. N. J. Dawood, translator. London: Penguin, 1956, 1990.

Devout Muslims did not like previous editions of this translation because the order of the *sura*s was shuffled to make it easier for the Western reader.

Wikeley, Lieut.-Colonel J. M. *Punjabi Musalmans*. Lahore: The Book House, 1986.

This short book, written by a British army officer in the 1930's and recently reprinted, contains a concise summary of Muslim beliefs, holidays, and ceremonies.

Chapter XII:
The Economy

The books by Emma Duncan and Richard Reeves, listed previously, were particularly valuable for this chapter. Some helpful statistical materials include:

Agricultural Statistics of Pakistan 1988–89. Islamabad: Government of Pakistan, Ministry of Food, Agriculture and Co-Operatives (Economic Wing).

Akhtar, Rafique. *Pakistan Year Book 1988–89*. Karachi: East and West Publishing Company.

Economic Survey 1988–89. Islamabad: Government of Pakistan, Finance Division, Economic Advisor's Wing.

Hamid Naved; Ijaz Babi; and Anjum Nasim. *Trade, Exchange Rate and Agricultural Pricing Policies in Pakistan*. Washington, D.C.: The World Bank, 1991.

Household Income Survey 1985–86. Karachi: Pakistan Federal Bureau of Statistics, November 1988.

Chapter XIII:
Food

Christine Osborne's book, listed previously, contains a short chapter on Pakistani cooking, followed by thirty recipes. Some other useful books include:

Singh, Balbir. *Indian Cookery*. New York: Weathervane Books, 1973.
   Likely to whet your appetite.

Solomon, Charmaine. *Indian Cooking for Pleasure*. New York: Chartwell Books Inc., 1978.
   Will whet your appetite further.

Chapter XIV:
Arts and Entertainment

The book by Donald M. Wilber, listed previously, offers a nice overview of Pakistani culture. Other more detailed books include:

Ahmad, Aijaz, editor. *Ghazals of Ghalib*. New York: Columbia University Press, 1971.
   An excellent translation of some of the best Urdu poetry of the nineteenth century.

Faiz, Ahmed Faiz. *The True Subject: Selected Poems of Faiz Ahmed Faiz*. Lazard, Naomi, translator. Princeton, N.J.: Princeton University Press, 1987.
   Because Ms. Lazard discussed these poems with Faiz Ahmed Faiz in detail, this is likely to remain the definitive translation of his mature work.

Harle, J. C. *The Art and Architecture of the Indian Subcontinent* (Pelican History of Art). Harmondsworth, England: Penguin Books, 1986.
   Informative chapters on Mughal painting and Indo-Islamic architecture.

Iqbal, Muhammad. *The Reconstruction of Religious Thought in Islam*. London: Oxford University Press, 1934.
   The great poet's famous lectures on the dynamic qualities of Islam.

Khan, Ahmad Nabi. *Muslim Art Heritage of Pakistan*. Islamabad: Pakistan

Directorate of Films and Publications, Government of Pakistan, 1989.

A paperback with concise text and beautiful photographs of the best architecture, calligraphy, and Mughal painting in Pakistan.

Chapter XV:
Education, Democracy, and the Future

Duncan, Ann, et al. *Women in Pakistan: An Economic and Social Strategy.* Washington, D.C.: The World Bank, 1989.

A detailed and gripping report on the role of women in Pakistan's economy and the inadequacy of the nation's educational and health facilities.

Pakistan and the World Bank. Washington, D.C.: The World Bank, 1985.

A short paperback on the economic and educational challenges facing Pakistan.

Qureshi, Muhammad Munir. *Fiscal Imperatives in Pakistan's Economic Development.* Lahore: Progressive Publishers, 1989.

A scholarly discussion of the narrowness of Pakistan's tax base and the corruption it causes.

Shami, Parwaiz. *Education in Search of Fundamentals.* Karachi: National Book Foundation, 1976.

Thirteen articles covering many aspects of education in Pakistan.

Filmography

Few Pakistani films are available in the United States. One American outlet for Urdu-language films is: Naghma House Ltd., 131 Lexington Avenue, New York, N.Y. 10016, tel. (212) 532–0770. What follows is a list of three Western movies about Pakistan and two Pakistani television shows. Most Pakistanis think their television dramas are better than their movies.

Gandhi —RCA/Columbia Home Video, 1982.

Many Pakistanis dislike this film because of its unflattering and rather unfair portrayal of Muhummad Ali Jinnah. In spite of this, the movie is an excellent account of Gandhi's role in India's struggle for independence from British colonialism.

Kim—MGM/UA Home Video, 1950.

A colorful movie based on Rudyard Kipling's delightful novel about an Irish orphan from the streets of Lahore who grows up to be a secret agent for the British.

The Man Who Would Be King—CBS/Fox Video, 1975.

A superb film based on Rudyard Kipling's short story about two British adventur-

ers who conquer Kafiristan, a valley in northernmost Pakistan, and briefly become
its rulers.

Dhoop Kinaray—in Urdu, Pakistan Television, 1981.
   A mini-series on four cassettes, this television serial is a gentle and subtle parody
   of day-to-day family relations in Pakistan.

Chakar-e-Azam—in Urdu, Pakistan Television, 1989.
   A mini-series on three cassettes, this serial drama is a portrayal of life and customs in a Punjabi village.

Discography

Music recorded in Pakistan may be found at Naghma House Ltd., previously mentioned in the Filmography. Here are two representative recordings in two different
styles, each on the EMI (Pakistan) Ltd. label (P.O. Box 3214, Karachi).

Folk (in Punjabi)

Mehmil and Other Hits by Musarrat Nazir, #TC-CEMCP-5935.

Pop (in Urdu)

Salma Agha and Mehdi Hassan, #TC-HMV-20086.

Index

Numbers in *italics* refer to illustrations.

146, 147, 175–76, 202–3
Sindhi, 39, 49, 206, 208
Sindhis, 27–30, 31, 124, 128, 206
Singh, Ranjit, 67
soap, 99
solar calendar, 48
soldiers. *See* army
songs, folk, 27, 208
Soviet Union, 6, 95, 118, 134, 182
Spector, Leonard, 114
spices, 59, 190–93
Srinagar, 92, 94
steel mills, 181
stone seals from Mohenjodaro, *45*
strikes, 100, 105
Sufism, 50, 160
sugar, 178
sugarcane, 19, 178
Sui gas fields, 17
Sulaiman mountains, 17
Sultana, Razia, 51
Sultanate of Delhi, 51–52
Sunni, xii, 160
Supreme Court, 126

Taj Mahal, 53, 61, 63
tandoor oven, *195*, 196
tanneries, 16
taxation, 52, 58–59, 63, 66, 186, 221–22
Taxila, 48–49
television, 39, 131, 154, 210–12
tenant farmers, 27, 175–76
textile mills, 71, 113, *180*, 181
Thakht-i-Bhai (Buddhist city), *48*
Thar Desert, 13, 27
tobacco, 19, 179
tomb, *28*, 53, 61, 66, 203
trade, foreign, 135
    See also exports, imports
transportation, 69–70, 147–48, *148*, *149*,
    153–54, 182
Tribal Areas of the Frontier, 11, 18, 32, 124
tube wells, 6, *8*, 10, 12, 14, 101

See also irrigation, water
two-party system, 133

ulema (clergy), 156, 171–73
unions, 128, 182–83
United Arab Emirates, 185, 211
United Nations cease-fire, 94
United States, 1, 2, 70, 101, 102, 117–19,
    126, 131, 185, 211, 212
universities, 72, 146, 220
uranium, 114–15
urban areas, 145–53
Urdu, xii, 4, 27, 29, 30, 35, 37–39, 43, 52,
    75, *78*, 92, 103, 200, 203, 204, 205,
    209, 219
Uzbeks, 55

Vedas, 47
vegetables, 143, 153, 179, 190, 192
veil, *169*, 170
videocassette players, 154, 211
villages, 50, 124, 137–44, 156, 168, 170
violence, religious, 50–51, 64–65, 85–88,
    91–92
voter registration, 126

wages, 100, 183, 184
Wakhan Corridor, 6, 20
warfare
    early, 46, 48–52, 55–57, 60, 64–67
    Post–World War II, 92–95, 102, 108–9,
    118, 135
water, 5, 135, 151–52, 168, 223
    wells, 71, 142
    See also canals, irrigation, pumps, tube
    wells
water buffalo, 138–41, *141*, 180
water jugs, *150*
Wavell, Lord, 82–83
Waziristan mountains, 19–20
Wazir Khan mosque, 200
Wazirs, 19–20
weddings, 165–67, *165*